Sergeant to CEO

*A Foster Kid's Lessons in
Family, Fidelity, and Financial Success*

by Sean P. Jensen

TRAITMARKER BOOKS

TRAITMARKER BOOKS
2984 Del Rio Pike
Franklin, TN 37069

Ordering Information for Quantity Sales
Special discounts are available on quantity purchases by corporations, associations, and others. For details, contact the author at the address above.

Attributions
Text Font: Minion Pro
Title Font: Minion Pro
Author Cover Photo: Keoni K.
Editors: Sharilyn Grayson, Mark Baird
Cover Design: Andrew Macarthur

Publisher's Data
Sergeant to CEO: A Foster Kid's Lessons in Family, Fidelity, and Financial Success
ISBN 978-1-944243-35-7
Published by TRAITMARKER BOOKS
traitmarkerbooks.com
traitmarker@gmail.com

Printed in the United States of America

Pau ka pali, hala

ka luuluu kaumaha.

(Past the precipice, past the fears)

ISBN 978-1-944243-35-7

Contents

Dedication

To my wife, Nicole, and my daughter, Charlotte:
I am so grateful that you allowed me into your lives. You have given me purpose and acceptance without condition. Thanks for your patience during this part of my journey, keeping me grounded when successful and pointing out the little things in life I can do better. The love and joy you have given me transcend all the accolades in my life. You two are my greatest triumph.

To my adopted family, my mother, Claudette, and my father, Larry:
I credit you with saving my young life and the lives of my sister, Kenna, and brother, Eric. Your intervention saved us from being lost without love and hope. I know that I was not easy to handle growing up. As trying as I was, please, know there is no end to my appreciation, and thanks for the way you gave us kids a second chance. I will never forget.

To my brothers and sisters:
We are all grown up now. I pray you will have a deeper understanding through my perspective of the boy I was and how I became the man I am today. I wish you all success and happiness in life.

To my biological mother:
Thank you for opening the door so late in life, allowing me to connect with my heritage and allowing me to find my true self by learning from the past.

Time does not change the past, but forgiveness can change the future.

Love always,
Your husband, father, brother, and son...

Sean Jensen
May 2015

Aloha

Hello

Preface

Sergeant to CEO describes the course I charted to success. I have been a CEO for over a dozen years, and I have gained a lot of knowledge and experience in my work. Much of my experience in understanding life and people came from serving in the US Marine Corps. I joined the Marines right out of high school, and they taught me valuable lessons about myself. They taught me how to lead, how to be led, and how to communicate with others from all walks of life. Even today, some 20 years later, the military is an intrinsic part of my life.

As far as *A Foster Kid's Lessons on Family, Fidelity, and Financial Success* goes, that brief title encapsulates my life story. It refers both to my business, Polu Kai Services, LLC, and to my Hawaiian heritage. You'll notice right away that the book you hold has a Hawaiian motif; that's because my identity as a Hawaiian is very important to me. The emphasis on family, on loyalty, and on persistence are all integral to who I am and why I've succeeded personally and in my business.

In business, people depend on you to honor your commitments. In the US Marine Corps, everything is well planned and organized to a T. Regiment and tradition are hallmarks of the Marines, especially the tradition of honor. Uniformity, discipline, codes, and rules guide your every day. These lessons have served me well.

While I am not the strapping young jarhead I used to be, I am still a force to be reckoned with. That's a good thing, because running a business requires a strong will to accomplish difficult tasks. If there is no driving force behind your business, it is almost certain to fail. As the founder, CEO, and "chief bottle washer" of my business, I am that force behind the scenes.

Before joining the Marines, I felt that I was always on the short end of the stick or bottom rung of the ladder. I was struggling in life, to say the least. At 17 years old, after a rough start, I had two paths in front of me. One path almost certainly led to life on the streets or to me bouncing from job to job. The possibility of spending some time in jail was down that road, too. The other path before me was a life in the military, where men and women would train me how to be a better person. All I had to do was make the right decision at the right time.

While my story is unique, it is not uncommon. Many people are not as fortunate as I was. Very few find a way out of the early childhood situations I faced and get a second chance. I received that second chance gift of adoption and acceptance into the USMC, and I firmly believe I have done all that I could with it.

Throughout this book, I will be blunt and straightforward. I don't want to sugar-coat the truth so that you end up reading a lie. This book is about my life and experience in entrepreneurship and about how important events shaped me into the CEO I am today. I want to show you some of the good decisions and bad decisions I made so that you can avoid the missteps I made on my way to success. I hope you will gain valuable insight as I explore my vision, ideas, values, success, and setbacks. I will share how I found the courage to succeed during times of chaos and confusion and how living life is, and has always been, my best teacher.

When I started my business, I had one really simple goal: Bring in more money than I sent out. I think anyone would agree that my goal was simply pure genius. What a concept!

But running a business is more complicated than my really simple goal. It's a series of choices that you have to make over time. Life is a long story with a new beginning every day. When I get up in the morning, I ask myself three questions: *Where did I get started? Where am I going? What am I doing today?*

A person without my responsibilities probably doesn't think of the answers to those questions regularly. As you take a shower, make breakfast, and then go off to school, work, sports practice, parties, meetings, or engagements, you're probably not thinking of your purpose in life: your core principles. But when you are a CEO, you really need to be able to answer these questions at a foundational level. You need to remind yourself of where you have been, especially if you don't want to go back to those places. You need to plan how and when you are going to travel the next distance along the way. Most importantly, you need to know where you want to go and what you are going to do when you get there.

You need to know the answers to these questions not only for yourself, but also for the people who follow you. I really cannot understate the value of committed employees. Business doesn't have to be hard. It should be fun. I love what I am doing and the impact I have on the world around me. I always said, "I can only control the sphere of influence around me. I can't think too hard about what my competitors are doing. I need to know what I am doing."

So the goal of this book is to share my story, my life lessons, and my own path to success from Sergeant to CEO. I hope that you can find inspiration from my pursuit of excellence and happiness.

Sean P. Jensen

Part One-

Ohana

Family

Sean P. Jensen

Chapter 1:

Setting Out on Rough Seas

Sean P. Jensen

MY real training for life and business began when I was six years old. I woke up in a motel in St. Petersburg, Florida, where my young mother, stepfather, brother, and baby sister were sharing one room. It was a bad situation, to say the least. We had a roof over our heads but little to eat. My mother worked as a maid at the motel, and my stepfather was a drunk and drug user.

While information is sketchy about how we ended up there, I have been told that my stepfather duped my mother into coming to Florida to start a new life where there was "work and opportunity."

It was the late 70s, and President Carter's administration was in full swing. Times were tough. Work was hard to come by. It was attainable if you tried; my mother demonstrated that. My stepfather probably could have found work. He just couldn't get off the drugs. And he was not a good drunk. Before too long, things turned violent, and representatives from the police and the Health and Human Services Department arrived.

All I knew was that some strange people showed up and whisked us kids away to foster care. The scene of 3 kids being taken is burned into my memory. The day they arrived was one of the two last looks I would get of my biological mother for a long time to come.

Sometime later, I saw my mother one more time. Thinking back, I can see by recalling her face that she did not seem well. She had a sad way about her, even though she was happy to see us kids. She told me that she was working on a plan and everything would be all right.

Unfortunately for me and my baby siblings, that plan never materialized. My caseworker showed up at the foster home sometime after that last meeting to tell me that my mother had missed her court dates and that no one was coming to get us. At 6 years old, I knew my life was forever changed.

The caseworkers then separated me from my brother and sister, putting us in different foster homes. They felt that the separation would give them a better chance to be adopted, because my age was a liability. Perhaps that move was well-meaning ignorance, or maybe it was institutionalized callousness. But it wasn't good for our family.

I knew deep inside, young as I was, that my brother and sister and I needed each other more now than ever. Our tragic loss had bonded us even further. We had lost so much that we couldn't lose any more. I felt a deep responsibility towards them and a passionate protectiveness.

So the decision to split us up did not go well for me. I fought back as well as a six year old could. I demanded that the social workers bring my siblings back to me. I pleaded, "They need me!" And I cried and screamed, "I need them!" I acted out and repeated these demands every day, insisting that the case workers reunite us.

The terror of being alone was overwhelming. Sometimes I would completely withdraw from the foster family. Sometimes I would get into physical altercations with the foster family's kids. When my siblings and I were put into separate foster homes, my world fell apart. The time without my brother and sister seemed like an eternity. They were sent one way, and I was sent another. They were too young to fight back. They had no voice at one and two years old. I was the only voice left.

I will never be sure if giving the foster family's boy a black eye led to our reuniting, but my message was clear: Bring them back to me. Eventually the social workers did reunite us. After a couple of months, all of a sudden they showed up at the foster home where I was staying. I was lucky. These trage- dies happen every day. I can only imagine what these social workers have to do just to get through a day. Having to do that job would be heartbreaking. But this experience led to my first *Sean life lesson: Speak up for yourself and others, even when it seems that no one will listen.*

When the social workers did bring my brother and sister back to me, I promised myself I would not let them out of my sight if I could help it. I was overjoyed. At least now I could take care of them and protect them. But my joy would be short. The reality of my situation was impossible for me to imagine. I had no family left but my two siblings, and my ability to care for them and protect them in my foster home was limited. I was saddened be- yond belief. I settled down and began the long wait for someone to help us. The foster home was purgatory. There was no love or affection, just sadness. Everything I knew in the world was wrong. Except for my siblings, everyone in the world that was important to me did not exist anymore. Our living situation was meager, sad, and hopeless.

The long-term foster home was a small, one-bedroom house that had a small addition built in front. Imagine a front porch extension without a screen. It was insulated, covered with wood and sheet rock, and split by a hallway to the front door. I shared one front room with my brother and sister, and the two kids from the foster family, who I will call Bob and Jane, took the other. We really didn't interact with Bob and Jane much; we were kept separate most of the time. The house had one bathroom that I had to ask permission to use. I was pretty much confined to the bedroom except for meals and some play time.

Bob and Jane were definitely higher on the family priority chain. I had to learn how to survive in that very unforgiving environment. Making matters worse, this family's idea of discipline and love was a belt. They were not scared to use it on me quite frequently. Whipping seemed to be a daily event. I was scared of the dad. Whenever he came home, the belt was sure to come out for reasons I can't even recall. So many emotions. On one hand, I was happy to have my brother and sister back. On the other hand, did I bring them into hell.

You could say we went from bad to worse. Sure, we were fed. We were given the bare minimum of clothes. But the most important thing we needed was love, and that was hard to come by. The parents already had two kids who were the most important people in this foster family's life. What could I, a six year old with two babies to protect, have done to deserve such hardship and neglect.

Two years had passed since my family's arrival in Florida, and sometime around my eighth birthday, I received a present: a meeting with a young married couple. She wore a dress, and he wore a suit and a tie. They had big smiles, and they seemed to care about me and my brother and sister. I'll admit; I was skeptical. *Who are these people?* I wondered. They took my siblings and me to lunch, and there was a buffet. I sampled nearly every dish at the Golden Corral that day. I loaded so much food on my plate that the strange man who took me there asked if I was going to eat it all. I told him yes. He smiled and said, "You shouldn't waste food." If he only knew how rare such a treat was! I wasn't going to waste a bite. At that point in my life, their visit was the best day ever.

Why were this man and woman being so nice? They must have felt very sorry for me. The caseworkers told them that I was un-adoptable because I was too old. And I could be trouble. I'd proved so in my demands for my siblings. Thank God for interventions, because the couple couldn't bear to leave me or take my brother and sister away from me. They had been looking for one special needs kid, and here were three kids with one special need: to stay together.

In January of 1981, a loving mother, Claudette, and a loving father, Larry, adopted me and my brother and sister. I will say this here and now: I am here today because of them. They cared enough to do what most people thought was insane: adopting three kids when they already had four! They went from a family of six to a family of nine! Who does that? But despite the great act of love my adoption was, I did not transition well. The memories of my past experiences were still there. As much as my new parents tried to help me, my heart was broken. I should have undergone counseling, but back then nobody really knew that kids with such a rough start needed therapy.

I had made no friends in foster care. I can't recall one, not one. Maybe making friends to most people is natural. It was not so with me. During the first year of adoption, all I wanted to do was stay in the house where I felt safe. I didn't have any friends except my brother and sisters. The problem at the time was hard to fathom for my parents. The real truth was that I didn't know how to make friends.

Finally one day, having had enough of me staying inside and hiding, my mother said to me, "Get outside, and ride your bike to the park! Make some friends. Don't come home until you do."

That push was exactly what I needed. It took me a couple of weeks, but I finally got the nerve to talk to the other kids. After a few months, I started developing relationships with other people. It was a small but important victory for me. I was not to experience equal victory in all areas of my new life.

Internally, I was very angry. I would tell stories that were not true, and I would hide food in my bedroom for fear that there would not be more where that came from, a habit I learned from the foster home. I had adopted a fake reality in the foster home to get through life. I guess I didn't realize that I had brought that baggage with me. I acted out quite a bit.

On top of that, there was a new hierarchy in this home. I went from being the oldest to being in the middle of the pack. I went from parenting to being parented. My adopted mother would chasten me when I tried to parent my younger siblings, telling me that it wasn't my job and she was the parent. We now had the freedom to be kids again. At the time, I wasn't sure how it would turn out. Understanding hierarchy and knowing where you stand on the planet is a very important skill, especially in the business world.

By our adoption, our new family expanded to four boys and three girls. Our ages ranged from three years old to fourteen years old. I don't know how my mother managed seven kids. Her learning curve in organizing all of us was interesting for everyone, to say the least. My adopted parents, Claudette and Larry, did their very best to educate us. They provided us with a stable, good home. Considering that I couldn't read at the second grade level, I was way below my age group in education. My adopted parents held me back a year so I could catch up. That along with speech therapy made me feel that I was starting to be like other boys again. There was a lot of love and a lot of discipline for me, but never a belt. There were values, religion, education, sports, Boy Scouts, piano, vacations, and camping. The full life we were living at that time was a change of fortune for some hardship kids like my brother and sister and me. I think that Claudette and Larry had some idea of what they were getting into when they adopted us, but they never could have imagined the difficulties ahead. Only later in life, as I became an adult, have I been able to tell them what really happened to us in a way I think they could fully comprehend. It is much easier to explain now that I am stable and can find the words.

Speaking of finding words, let me tell you that I have never written a book before. As I kid, I was told I had ADHD, and the doctors in my life treated me with Ritalin. They stopped after they saw the effect on my personality. As an adult, I claim I have ADHD in High Definition. The truth is that I have always struggled with focusing my energy, ever since I was young boy. But now instead of a liability, I think of my ADHD in HD as an asset. I actually think it helped me better focus on simultaneous, high-pressure events that all needed my attention at once.

Another truth I learned about myself as a child is that I'm not afraid of work. When I was 8 years old, I set up "Sean's Snake-Catching Service." My mom put an advertisement in the Village Voice, and the ladies from around the neighborhood would call her to get me to catch snakes in their yards. I would catch them and then ride my bike 5 miles to the pet store and sell the snakes to them. Back then, everyone wanted a corn snake or red rat snake. I made a killing. After that, I mowed lawns at 10 years old, washed dishes at 14, and bagged groceries at 15 while I was a bar-back at an Italian restaurant at night. Whether or not I was mowing lawns or bussing tables, I was working hard before I joined the Marines. I was always a good worker. I guess my entrepreneurial spirit started much earlier than I thought.

One of my favorite jobs back then was being the parts salesman at Western Auto. I rode my bike (my mode of transportation back then) over to the new Western Auto parts store being built. It was like a super box store for automobiles, a flagship store for the company's arrival in Florida. When I walked in the door, some employees were stocking the shelves and preparing for a major grand opening. There were two serious men in ties at the front office with name tags. I figured that they were in charge.

I walked over to them, said, "Good afternoon," and asked them for a job. A little intrigued, they both looked at me. Mr. Charles, a graying fellow, was both the store president and the area president. He sized me up.

I am laughing thinking about it now. Here's this 16-year-old kid who doesn't know how to change the oil in a car asking for a job at an auto parts store!

Mr. Charles asked me what I knew about auto parts, and I admitted, "I do not know anything right now, but I could learn. I could help stock these shelves, and I would know where to find everything. I can start work today!"

Impressed by my answer, Mr. Charles had no choice but to hire me on the spot. I started right then and there stocking shelves. In a year's time, I became a top tire salesman as a part-timer. I earned as much as an extra hundred dollars every two weeks in tire commission sales. For me, earning a living was natural. I applied myself in all my endeavors, no matter what I felt about any of my jobs. I've never been afraid to work.

But somewhere in my teen years, I began acting out again. My parents struggled with me. The older I became, the greater my problems with authority became. I ran away a few times and was even kicked out of the house at one point. My choices may not make sense to you, but the turmoil inside me kept me from following the status quo in front of me. I began living on the streets, going back home, and heading out on the streets again.

I dropped out of sports during my senior year in high school. Most kids were planning to go to college or to do something with their lives. Not me. I was busy blaming the world for my problems and feeling sorry for myself. I couldn't wait to grow up and make my own decisions. I was in a constant state of confusion, partly because I was going through life not knowing who I was. I never really felt like I belonged anywhere, even though I was told I belonged to my adopted family. I didn't understand why I couldn't get over the past. The older I got, the worse my feelings of anger and loneliness and my resulting behavior became.

The memories of my biological parents, who were physically long gone from my life, were still inside my mind and my soul. They broke their trust when they abandoned me and my siblings, and that memory of broken trust stayed with me, even after I was adopted. The foster home and the tragic separation from my brother and sister as a youth never left me. Those haunting memories and terrible feelings weren't my adopted parents' fault. They tried to help me belong and adjust. But I would have to solve the mystery of who I was and where I belonged for myself.

Anger continued to consume me. I had a few brushes with the law, nothing major, just juvenile stuff. However, deep inside of me I knew that I had to find a way to break the cycle of sorrow and self-pity. I needed to discover who I was. At that point, I needed the Marine Corps more than the Marine Corps needed me. All I had to do was finish high school, and I would be home free. I barely did it.

In a way, I was a recruiter's dream. I met with all branches of the military, trying to figure out where to go. When I saw that poster of a Marine in full dress blues touching his sword to his white hat brim, I was hooked. That's all it took. I wanted to be that guy. As far back as I can remember, I had two life goals: to be president of something, and to be GI Joe.

Parris Island Marine Recruiting Station was a good start for me. I signed up for the eight-year program: six years active duty with two years in the Marine Reserves. I would be 24 before I had to reenlist. At the time, eight years seemed like an eternity to me. I knew in my heart that truly changing would take me all of the time I could get. I vowed to reinvent myself and put the painful past behind me, along with my personal pity party.

When I got to Parris Island, South Carolina, the famous yellow footprints painted across the asphalt road leading to the recruit depot greeted me. They represented the millions of recruits who had arrived before me. At the time, I wasn't sure where I was going or what I was going to do, but the footprints directed me to my next step. I knew only that they led to boot camp and that I would need to graduate from there to become a U.S. Marine.

Meanwhile, the rumor mill churned back home; I heard that there was a betting pool as to whether or not I would make it. If you tell me that I can't do something, and I will move mountains to prove you wrong or to show you I can. My relatives didn't understand then what I already did: that you can make a lot of bad decisions in life but all it takes is one good one to change your destiny. Joining the Marines was my first truly good decision.

I also learned that when you make decisions, timing is very critical. Being a Marine was not going to be an easy task. I told myself that if I survived boot camp, training, and six years' active duty in the USMC, I would then surely know what I wanted to do with my life. I kept my Marine Corps goal simple: to obtain the rank of corporal and learn all I could.

The message I want to share with you in detailing my life is this: set achievable goals. In high school, I looked at my situation and recognized where I was and the two paths that lay ahead of me. By joining the Marines, I learned what I needed to do to get to the next level.

Getting to the next level was not fun or easy. In boot camp, it was drill, knowledge, physical strength, and most importantly, mental toughness. My butt was kicked. I was run into the ground, and I had to fight hard in every phase of training. I had an attitude, an identity crisis, and a truckload of mental baggage that I couldn't let go. And I wasn't the only one.

We new recruits with attitudes all had our reasons. I remember similar stories from guys going through training with me, young men from all walks of life. Every part of the country was represented.

For me, I took what I learned in foster care to heart. I would keep to myself and try and blend in. I decided that keeping a low a profile was the best way to avoid the drill instructors. To my dismay, they were very good at getting a piece of everyone, including me. The US Marine Corps is an equal opportunity employer when it comes to getting reamed out. The drill instructors would have you believe you couldn't do anything right. Recruits learned quickly that the Marine way of doing everything was the only way of doing anything.

Some days were what we called in boot camp "chow to chow" or "meal to meal." It was just like at the foster home: getting through a day by taking it hour by hour, meal by meal. Remember, small achievable goals. The only difference here was that I had help and that, maybe for the first time, people wanted me to succeed. The drill instructors saw to our well-being, and they encouraged us through the work. Mentally, I had to separate training evolutions by meals; otherwise, it would have been difficult to survive 13 weeks of "boot." It reminded me of the foster home in another way, too: I had to get past the belt to go to bed.

I quickly learned that the Marines do something very well. They strip the individual down to the bone, mentally removing the individuality. The process is a real eye opener. You are not allowed to say "I" but only "this recruit." You always speak in the third person. They teach you how to become a warrior, an amphibious green monster, a member of a team. I graduated boot camp and entered the service as a person much more in control of himself.

After a couple of years in the service, I was a young lance corporal, just coasting along. I had the system down pat. I was living in Norfolk, Virginia, having completed my post-boot-camp training at Camp Lejeune. My first duty station allowed me to begin enjoying the night life after work days on base. Virginia Beach was right down the road, and there was a party or a club every day of the week. Norfolk, a huge Navy town, had no shortage of bars and girls. So I would work all day and party all night. I wasn't alone in that lifestyle. We Marines were young, and we stuck together. I was enjoying new freedoms the fleet Marine Corps offered. With weekend liberty and nightlife, I almost felt like a civilian. I wasn't being monitored 24 hours a day like I was in training.

One evening as I was getting ready to hit the club scene, this veteran staff sergeant came up to me and firmly grabbed the back of my neck to get my undivided attention. His voice fluctuating in pitch, he said, "You jenky motherfucker! I've been watching you. You think you got it all figured out, don't you?"

His name was SSgt. Featherston. His friends called him "Fed" or "SSgt Fed." Lance corporals like me called him Staff Sergeant. I had not earned the friend part yet. After all, he was three ranks higher than me, a lowly E-3. He was living in the barracks due to a recent move. It wasn't uncommon to see senior Marines move in to our home. Normally the barracks were reserved for E-6 SSgts. and below. The Marines who moved back had usually made a bad marriage decision or tried to live out in town on our low pay.

SSgt was a tall, skinny, 6' 2" brother from Newport News, VA. He was a guy you didn't want to piss off: spit and polish, uniforms starched and pressed. He knew his job, and I knew that I didn't want to get in his way. He was what we younger guys would call a squared away Marine. Not that I wasn't squared away - I was just young and new to the Corps. He was a salty sea dog. At first when I saw him in the barracks, I thought, *Great, so much for leaving guys like him at work.* I saw him every day, nights and weekends. So his living in the barracks led to our discussion. He had been watching us, the young lance corporals partying in town, specifically me. And this night, he decided to get involved.

"What do you mean, Staff Sergeant?" I replied.

"Why don't you want to get promoted, Lance Corporal?"

"I would love to get promoted, Staff Sergeant," I told him. "It just seems like a lot of responsibility. I am doing fine. I'll get there eventually."

That's when he gave me the news flash: I wasn't doing fine. He told me that I was falling behind by not continuing to educate myself and commit to self-improvement (personal goals I had forgotten). The Staff Sergeant told me, "You are never going to get promoted the way you are going!" Then he asked me, "Do you want to become a leader, or are you going to be an arrogant jackass for the rest of your life?"

"No, SSGT!" I responded abruptly. "I want to be a leader!"

That was my good life decision number two. My simple answer in the affirmative created an opportunity for me to learn from this 18-year USMC veteran. He wasted no time beginning my education.

"If you work for the Marine Corps," he explained, "it will work for you." He told me that he was once like I was. He did not want to see me go down that same path, being so young. He would train me. And if I didn't meet his expectations, he would personally see me out of his Marine Corps.

Little did I know then that this man was going to be my first mentor. He was going to change me. He could see potential in me that I couldn't see. I was blind to any avenues relating to my future and success. How did he know?

The young Marines all looked up to the higher ranks. It was only natural. In his case, I imagine he knew his time would be over soon, and he wanted to affect the younger guys before he left. After I committed to him, he volunteered me for everything, including leadership training and advanced courses in Marine Corps education. He would interrupt my personal time and conduct inspections on me. Sometimes he would hold a Saturday 7 PM inspection to slow me down on the partying. At other times, he would quiz me on Marine Corps history and knowledge. But most importantly, he taught me how to be a better Marine by taking the basic principles we learned in boot camp and expounding on them. He was my "Sea Daddy" as they like to call mentors in Naval Service. And because this US Marine Staff Sergeant saw something in me, I was on my way to becoming a better Marine and a better man. I don't know where SSgt Fed is today, but I will always be indebted to him. (If you're reading this, SSgt: Thanks.)

I ended up going to school on SSgt Fed's recommendation to become a primary marksmanship instructor. I began giving back, just as he said I would. As a lance corporal, I was trained to teach the most important knowledge Marines are famous for: marksmanship. Every Marine is a rifleman first.

I was definitely gaining ground with my SSgt around. Unfortunately, I got new orders, and my life changed again. This time, I was sent to Japan. But even there, I continued to develop myself. Every chance I had, I trained and took professional courses of all types. I was growing up. Three and a half years and counting in the service, I was becoming a veteran and a leader.

I started evolving overseas. I started to get a mind of my own. Thanks to the admonitions and instructions of that SSgt, I was promoted to corporal. I had met my Marine Corps goal.

But then I stalled. And one of the problems with stalling is that other people notice. I had a few run-ins in Okinawa with a gunny and a 2nd lieutenant who seemed to have something against me. I'll call them Frick and Frack. I admit, I had a bit of an attitude because I didn't like the way those two ran together. Both of them were black, and they definitely did not like white folks, even if those white folks were Marines. They let me know how they felt about Florida crackers like me and the few other Marines in their charge that were not in their club. Yes, there was still discrimination in the military on both sides of the spectrum.

I did not view color like that. I was brought up right. The way Frick and Frack treated their subordinates discouraged me. I didn't believe them to be fair. I didn't see how they could be out playing basketball, fraternizing with the ranks, calling each other by first names, and then effectively command.

I ignore color, and I always have. The way I regard people has much more to do with their actions. Personally, I don't care if you are white, green, black, or purple: I was not brought up a racist. All I cared about was doing my job

21

without interference. The Marines had policies in place to keep good order and discipline. I always kept my respect for senior-ranking Marines. I wasn't an 18-year salty vet, but I knew bad leaders when I saw them. Frick and Frack didn't represent the Marine Corps leadership in my mind. They were nothing like SSgt. He was black, but he was not prejudiced. We were all Marines; color was not an issue to him. Job performance was how he gauged his men. He was a true leader.

When a piece of wood fell off my truck while I was driving around Okinawa, my two antagonists pressed charges against me. The wood scratched a car driven by a Japanese civilian. There were no injuries or major damage; so for any other Marine, there would have been only an accident report. Since it was me, Frick and Frack pressed for kicking me out of the Marine Corps

The company commander received the details of the incident. He asked me what happened. I was honest and admitted that I could have tied the wood down better. He chided Frack at the hearing. He was not impressed by these types of charges. He gave me barracks restriction for 14 days, supporting the higher-ranking Frack because of my admission. To me, it was clear that Frick and Frack were out to ruin my career. I would need to avoid them.

Thankfully, I ended up working in a battalion-level billet handling the disposal of hazardous waste while going to professional schools. No one wanted the job, so I took it. It got me away from Frick and Frack, who then tried to get me back for dodging their bullet. In their chain of command was a battalion sergeant major who saw what was going on. He stopped them. But Frick and Frack never saw any punishment for their behavior. I felt sorry for the Marines left in their command.

A year overseas was a great experience for me. It also was one of the loneliest times in my life. I did a lot of soul searching as I planned my future. I just wanted to avoid everyone. I had nearly zero communication with everyone back home. Some of my family didn't even know I was overseas. I shared not one phone call or letter back home.

While I was in Okinawa, I studied Japanese. I learned about the culture and mingled with the population. Besides a few military operations, my duties were pretty benign. The best part of the work overseas was learning a new trade. In the early 90s, environmental protection was really on the radar. The hazardous waste disposal business was fun for me, while it was complicated for many others.

I recognized the possibilities and listened to Marines I respected about hazardous material/waste disposal career potentials outside the military. When I got to back Quantico Marine Base for my final tour, I was two and half years from reenlistment, but I knew that I was not going to reenlist. I felt a different calling in life; I just didn't know what it was going to be yet. Knowing that I wanted to change directions, I did something unusual. I asked for a different assignment. As an unwritten rule, you go where the Marines tell you for your first enlistment. I didn't know if that was really true; so I tried to change my duty assignment anyways. It worked!

In the beginning of my enlistment, I was an infantryman until an injury changed that job to motor transport. During my time with SSgt Fed, I trained and certified as a Marine Corps primary marksmanship instructor.

This accomplishment qualified me to go to Quantico's legendary rifle ranges to teach weapons. Quantico was known for its shooting teams and Officers Candidate School. I had worked with the fleet anti-terrorism teams (FAST) as a primary marksmanship instructor, and I enjoyed every minute of that time. Transfer there could have been an option in my request. However, I saw no future in being a gunslinger, and I didn't want to go to the motor pool, my other military operational specialty (MOS). I didn't want to be a bus driver when I returned to civilian life.

I had done what I set out to do from the beginning of my enlistment. I made corporal, and I learned 3 MOSs, exceeding my own expectations. There was an opportunity to earn a fourth MOS as a certified hazardous material hazardous waste specialist, an MOS that was relatively new to the Corps at the time. That job was what I could see myself doing for the rest of my life: being involved in the hazardous waste material disposal field. My thought process was simple. There will always be chemical spills on the planet that needed cleaning up. I could build a career with my newfound knowledge. Smart decision three: attempt to influence destiny.

When I asked my career planner if I could make a lateral move into an environmental assignment, she told me that there was a billet open that was reserved for a higher rank. Nevertheless, she would be willing to make the change to my orders if I could get myself hired.

That day, I went in for an interview and met my last commanding officer, Major Fred Mock. I was nervous, because here was my chance to train for my permanent career. As I stepped into the office, I stood at attention and waited for the major to acknowledge my presence. He waved me in and motioned for me to take a seat. I noticed that he was reviewing my service record book. I wasn't sure what he was thinking. After all, being in an environmental MOS really wasn't cool. The other Marines ribbed me when I was doing that kind of work in Japan. I always shrugged off the taunts. A Marine who was out protecting the environment did not seem very manly to some other Marines.

Major Mock asked me why I wanted to work for environmental affairs. I told him the truth. "I want to educate myself in the environmental programs as a civilian career. I do not see myself being a 20-year Marine veteran, sir. And the skill sets I need to learn in order to become a civilian employee prospect are there if you will allow me to serve under you. Besides, I actually like the work." None of what I said seemed to bother him.

"You're hired!" he told me after briefly sizing me up. "I'll let the master guns know to approve the transfer." He dismissed me.

I stood at attention and marched out smiling inside. *I have a new job!* I thought. *Awesome! Better make the best of this opportunity. After all, you asked for it, Sean.*

Right then and there, I considered the major to be my mentor number two, right after SSgt Fed. He just didn't know it then.

My new job and final permanent assignment with the Marines involved emergency chemical spill response and clean up. I briefed commanders on environmental issues, trained Marines on environmental stewardship, and worked with the state of Virginia and the Environmental Protection Agency (EPA) on environmental compliance issues for the Marines. This job also gave me my first experiences dealing with federal civilian employees.

The Marines desperately needed trained specialists in this position because the EPA was clobbering the military. The job I had taken wasn't popular or glorious, and nobody else really wanted it. Admittedly, we US Marines had not been the best protectors of the environment, but much has changed since the founding of the EPA. After all, our primary mission was to fight.

When I took the assignment, my fellow Marines gave me a hard time. They called me an amphibious green peace monster. There were also some unhappy unit commanders who found out they were going to be a body short because of my transfer request and approval from base headquarters.

The Marine I replaced (I'll call him Bulldog) was a gunnery sergeant and something of a hazmat guru. Bulldog was very smart, but my new coworkers informed me that he was also a bit of an asshole. I took the hint. I told myself, *Keep your mouth shut, your eyes open, and listen and learn!*

Bulldog hadn't made too many civilian friends. But I had been put in a senior staff non-commissioned officer (NCO) billet. That kind of favor is not normally shown to NCOs, who usually obtain their position of authority by promotion through enlisted ranks. In other words, this job was a big step for a 22-year old Marine, and I had to be careful not to get a big head like Bulldog. I wanted to make plenty of new friends, though I was prepared to encounter a few unintentional enemies like Frick and Frack, too.

And now I also had civilian bosses. Since I was new to the field and low man on the totem pole, pretty much everyone was my boss. Basically, I accepted being treated like a private again.

Regardless, I embraced the new position. Training in chemical suits and learning about the many different chemicals that could kill you was quite a rush. The major looked out for me, but he also worked my butt off. The major made sure that I had the best training, and he helped me develop as a person and a civilian as well. He was genuinely interested in my success and growth. I knew that as long as I gave 100%, he would do what he could to benefit me. So I made sure I did a great job every day. I reckoned he had enough politics on his plate with the federal civilians he had to handle, as well as the commanders who didn't want to hear about environmental issues that could get them thrown in jail. For me, this job was a great responsibility and one that I knew I could not fail. The last thing the major needed was for me to be labeled a problem Marine by the civilians working there.

I did every job as I was directed to do, without fail. My primary job encompassed a broad spectrum of activities: prevent pollution on base; manage and store thousands of pounds of chemicals for proper disposal; respond to chemical spills around the base; interact with federal and state environmental regulators; work to reduce fines and violations by keeping Marine units in compliance with federal, state, and local environmental laws; and much more. Finally, my favorite duty was teaching my fellow Marines to be better stewards of the environment. I did all of the above.

I am proud to say that the major's unit received many commendations and letters from the commanding general. We were able to turn the tide on the number of pollution violations that were severely impacting the base. Our compliance inspections and proper storage of hazardous waste and materials grabbed attention. I am sure that we saved the Marine Corps hundreds of thousands and maybe millions of dollars. While I was working with environmental affairs, I took pride in knowing that I was a small part of the solution. The knowledge I gained proved to be useful and extensive. I ended up graduating in one of the first classes of the hazardous material waste specialist MOS. The major also made sure that I was recommended for promotion to sergeant for my efforts. Exceeding my original goals in joining the Marine Corps gave me confidence. I felt that I was really starting to find myself, and I was having fun in my career.

Chapter 2:

I'm Going to Need a Bigger Boat

Sean P. Jensen

DURING my final tour, one other important life-changing event occurred: I met a great woman. We have all heard the saying, "Behind every man is a good woman." Times have changed a bit, and that saying could go either way these days. This woman wasn't behind me; she was next to me. And that's exactly what I needed.

I had succeeded at changing my career path in the Marines. Now I asked myself, *Can I be successful at having a family?* I had been in a few relationships throughout my short Marine life. I'd had a girlfriend in high school, one in Japan, and one in Virginia Beach. None of them were like the woman I found now.

I still struggled personally. I had a maturity issue. I blamed the family from my past for many of my problems, and I wasn't ready mentally for personal challenges early in my career. I wasn't ready for any additional commitment then.

I make no apologies for not being ready, though. Many people in their twenties aren't ready for serious commitment. I can't count the number of failed military marriages I witnessed in the US military because young people couldn't gauge their own maturity and readiness to embrace commitment.

But thanks to SSgt Fed, I'd spent my time as a Marine gathering life intelligence from around the world. I was learning to respect other cultures and discovering the keys to success along the way. I'd matured in that way.

Still, I was pretty stubborn and could barely manage myself personally. My finances were a wreck; I was living paycheck to paycheck in the barracks. I really wasn't sure how I could support a family in the Marines or immediately post-military service. I never contemplated that responsibility. First, the pay was pretty bad; you don't join the military for the pay.

Mostly, though, I didn't want to fail like my stepfather. Remember the guy I mentioned earlier? The one who dragged my biological mom, brother, sister, and me to Florida without a clear path? I was very scared of repeating that horrible situation.

At the beginning of my Quantico tour, I began hanging out with a Marine buddy who was just back in the United States like me. We checked into the base together. He was from Texas (I'll call him Tex), and he had just returned from embassy duty. He liked to hit this country bar called Blackies in Springfield, VA. Though it's gone now, back then that country bar was Tex's

29

life. I had a car, and because all he wanted to do was go there, that's where we usually ended up. He liked to chase girls in tall hats, tight jeans, and cowboy boots. I wore blue jeans, hiking boots, and a collared shirt. In other words, I didn't fit in with the other country customers.

Now don't get me wrong; I liked chasing girls. I just wasn't much of a country two-step kind of guy, and this bar was filled with girls looking for guys who wanted to dance with them. Little did I know that one night in February 1996, one of those two-stepping princesses would steal my heart and change my future.

One night, Tex was trying to pick up a lady named Kim. Attempting to keep me from leaving, Tex introduced me to Kim's sister Nicole. She was there to take Tex's new friend Kim home, while Tex wanted to dance and party the night away with Kim. Summoning up the courage, I asked Nicole to dance. I didn't know at the time that she had just come back from a bad blind date and was not really looking to deal with a bundle of problems like me at the moment. So when I asked her to dance, she checked me out from head to toe and asked, "Do you know how?" Confidently, I said yes. We got on the dance floor, where I promptly stepped all over her feet. She was unimpressed by my dancing skills but quietly shook off her disappointment. Undeterred, I convinced her to hang out for a bit. It seemed that Tex and Kim were good with that.

Nicole could tell that I wasn't much of a cowboy. I couldn't two-step my way out of a wet paper bag. She was a redhead wearing Wrangler jeans with Justin boots and Stetson hat. She and Kim were from the local area, and they loved to come out and dance at Blackies. I was smitten by her.

As the night progressed, I quickly realized that there was something different about this woman. She had maturity and confidence. She knew who she was. The more we talked, the less we danced. During our conversation, I could see her as a counter balance to my conquer-the-world attitude. She got me to do something no other girl had done before: pay attention.

I didn't know it on the dance floor, but my plans to do everything I could in life and see what happened were going to meet personal responsibility and family obligations. They say that opposites attract. She was my perfect opposite! To this day, I call her the balance to my force.

What started as a night at a country bar ended up as a Denny's breakfast with this lovely lady and her sister. I'd had too much to drink after a good, long night of partying. As we sat at Denny's, I wanted to eat everything on the menu. I probably should have stuck to the eating, because I ended up saying something foolish.

"I am so glad I met you. I am tired of meeting divorced women with kids," I said while opening my mouth for a big bite of pancakes.

Nicole and her sister started laughing at me. I was so embarrassed that I nearly choked on my food. I knew I had said something wrong.

My soon-to-be ex date (or so I thought) replied, "Well, I am divorced, and I have a four-year-old daughter."

She said this with seriousness while laughing at me for my thoughtless comment. She was no stranger to military guys. There were four bases within 50 miles. I was pretty red with embarrassment. I apologized profusely. What was I thinking? Lucky for me, she was also wired with an incredible sense of humor and a very easygoing personality.

Talk about karma. What a sobering life moment.

I really liked this young lady, and I thought I had screwed it up in one sentence. Thank the Lord, she had a sense of humor and was attracted to this young Marine just as much as I was to her. We officially began dating, and I started hanging out with her and her daughter Charlotte more and more.

Our courtship would progress quickly. I fell hook, line, and sinker for her. About three weeks after we met, I traveled to Ft. Sill, Oklahoma for some training that would last for a month. We were still dialing home numbers back then; I didn't have a cell phone.

While I was in Oklahoma, I called Nicole one night from my room at the base hotel and told her I loved her. She kind of giggled and just said okay, and then we said good night. She thought I had been drinking too much. I'd had a few drinks in me to gather the courage, but I meant it.

Nicole managed to wait the month for my return without bringing up my words again. She was at the airport waiting for me when I got back, and she wanted to see if I remembered saying I loved her. I did. I knew in that moment that I wanted to marry this woman.

Yes, you're doing the math right. I was about to propose to this woman that I hadn't even known for three months.

I had one slight problem. Thanks to my excellent financial skills, I was too broke to buy a ring with savings alone. I was already working part-time at a Pep Boys auto store as a parts salesman. The extra money helped; I had begun moonlighting after work to catch up on bills. It was not too uncommon for enlisted guys to take a second job in garrison if they could. How was I going to pull such a huge purchase off? I didn't know; so I asked for help.

Tim, one of Nicole's friends, was just the guy to ask. He was a problem solver in the literal sense, and I trusted him. He was a great guy who's still a friend to this day. At the time he was an active duty member of the Air Force, a pretty seasoned staff NCO. He knew how much money a corporal had. I believe I could lay my hands on a mere $200 at the time. Tim assured me that despite my lack of funds, we could make it work and get the ring. I appreciated his encouragement, but I still thought I was going to need a miracle to buy this ring. Well, a miracle I got.

A month or so before Mother's Day, a store down the road was having a going-out-of-business sale. On top of that, they had sent mailers out with a scratch card that held three possible hidden discounts. Tim had picked up one, and he handed it to me. I needed all of the help I could get.

By good fortune, I was able to win the 30% off discount to buy a wedding ring. I still had to apply for a high APR in-store credit card. The store was going out of business, and the ring itself was $1,400. But with the Mother's Day sale price reduction plus the scratch card, the ring came to $701 dollars. Applying for the in-store card, I was approved for $700 dollars in credit. Imagine that!

The catch to buying the ring was that I would need a dollar to get started. I did not have another dollar. Tim opened his wallet and handed me the $1. It was a seize-the-moment opportunity. I don't think I ever repaid that debt. Someday, I will have to ask him if he wants his dollar back. It allowed me to marry the girl of my dreams.

Three weeks later, I went on bended knee and asked her to marry me. She said yes right away, and my heart was so full that I wanted to give her the world. "Nicole, don't worry. I am going to be a millionaire by the time I'm 30." I doubt that she believed me, but she jumped into the marriage. I was the happiest man alive! Little did I know that I had her at being "tired of meeting divorced women with kids."

I had no regrets asking her to be my wife. But I had one more obstacle on my way down the aisle. I had to get past Nicole's dad, Gordon, to finalize the agreement. I am a traditional guy, and I knew I would have to ask him for her hand in marriage. Gordon was seventy years old. I was sure he would appreciate the tradition. A retired business owner and master plumber, he was a very interesting guy. I had met him a few times prior to this event.

Admittedly, I was nervous. This was the first time I had ever approached a potential father-in-law like this. I wasn't sure what to expect from him. He was graying with a bald spot on his head. He was also very meticulous and astute, a craftsman with analytical eyes. Nicole warned me that Gordon would not make things easy for me. Arriving at his house, I walked in to find him at his favorite chair, watching television. After a couple of pleasantries, I just came out with it.

"Mr. Gordon, I would like to marry your daughter."

He didn't answer immediately. Instead, he had a question for me. I was befuddled when he asked it. "Sonny, what makes the world go around?"

I answered, "Money."

"Wrong, Sonny," he said. The one-word answer he gave me began with a "P." You can speculate on what word the "P" stood for. My jaw hit the floor. Did the father of my future wife just say that?

I was stunned. But thinking back, I believe he may have been right. After some explanation that I won't repeat here, he said yes and welcomed me to the family. He was very happy that his little girl would have a new protector, a Marine of all people.

I was fond of him, but he could be very pointed in his description of people and life. It took me some time to get used to him and his demeanor. Gordon was good man, a product of the Great Depression. He became a valued advisor for me in life. He liked me, even though we disagreed on everything, especially politics. We did agree on the most important thing: that we both loved Nicole and Charlotte. The other thing we agreed on was that the only way to achieve success in life is hard work and perseverance, just as he had done with his life and plumbing business and as I planned to do with my new skills in environmental protection.

My new step-daughter, Charlotte, was 4 years old at the time, so close to the age I had been when I was abandoned. I always called her yahoo. She would smile and say, "I'm not a yoohoo!"

She was a sweet young lady. I wondered if I would be a good father. Would I be a good provider? I had seen the best in my adopted dad and the worst with my stepfather and foster father. Time would tell what kind of father I would be. For now, I really felt I had a place and a future with this family of my own. I had a new reason to survive and make life work.

My opportunity to succeed had started when Larry and Claudette pulled me and my siblings out of hell, adopting 3 lost kids. My decision to join the Marines created more opportunity. Any success I had gained after that point of my life began with SSgt Fed, the guy who grabbed me by the scruff of my neck and gave me the advice that I needed when I was content to be just a lance corporal. Since that day, my growth, experience, and the knowledge I'd gained in service had helped me become a man.

Now my new wife and daughter brought balance and responsibility to me. I seemed to mature overnight. Time progressed pretty quickly. I started planning my exit from service. I had mastered four MOSs, attended numerous professional schools, and received a promotion to sergeant. When the Marine Corps asked me to reenlist, I dutifully declined. I knew that I was ready to sail my bigger boat on different seas.

Chapter 3:

Goodbye, Globe and Anchor

Sean P. Jensen

THE symbol of the Marine Corps is a globe in front of an anchor with an eagle over them. The globe stands for willingness to serve in any part of the world. The anchor stands for the long tradition of the naval service where the Marines have their roots. The eagle stands for the United States. And though I was still loyal to the United States and thankful for the Marine Corps, I no longer wanted to sail to any corner of the globe, because my family was my new anchor in life. My priorities had changed. I had a beautiful wife with a young stepdaughter. I was 25 years old. What's next? I asked myself. I was eager to find out.

I was done with my military service. I had a new direction professionally, too. Chemical spills and environmental problems were a boom industry, and I was certain that with my education, training, and immense experience in hazmat in the Marine Corps, that work should be easy for me to find. This future would allow me to find sustainable work and decent pay. There was a market for me. I didn't have a college degree, but I had mastered a profession with hands-on experience. I knew that I was going to do something special.

The Marines were an important port of call in my life's journey. I'd traveled a long way getting where I was now, and I'd steered my ship wrong a few times. But I made the right important decisions at the right times. I thank the guardian angels that were sent to help me, because enduring my early childhood challenges made me strong and a force to be reckoned with. I was still dealing with my past, but now I was dealing with it as a confident man. Success was around the corner; I just had to create new opportunities to find it.

I was planning my exit from the Marines the day I got to Quantico. About six months prior to being discharged, I sent resumes to every job announcement I saw in the environmental field. I thought that doing this would make me relevant and give me early exposure to the job market. My thinking process was simple: if I didn't get the job right away, it would be fine. I assumed that there would be some sort of process, and I would land a gig to time my exit with my terminal leave, double dipping to give my family some extra dough. I had a couple of prospects in no time.

Unfortunately, the majority of the companies who interviewed me didn't want to hire me. And their reluctance wasn't due to my qualifications and experience.

Human Resources (HR) departments had position requirements. If those requirements weren't met, the company was not going to hire me. Many of the jobs were working on environmental cleanup sites and taking environmental samples in the field. How hard could taking dirt and water samples be? The EPA had trained me on everything I needed to know regarding taking hazardous material samples. Why wasn't my real-world experience good enough? It seemed that no matter where I went, each company had a reason why it wouldn't hire a guy whose last six years of life had been spent on active duty. I had two things working against me. One, I had no college degree. Two, I had no civilian job experience.

The way I looked at the situation was that even if I had a degree in something useless like basket weaving, it would be good enough because of my experience. What does "honorably discharged United States Marine sergeant" mean to employers anyway?

Months went by. I came ever closer to ending my Marine career. I struggled with my future. What was I going to do? I had no other job prospects at all. Finally, about two weeks before I was to start my final paid vacation days as a Marine, I got a call and landed a job.

I was going to be an environmental recruiter, not a hazmat waste specialist. But this recruiter job would be a start. "Job One" as I called it, began with a two-week boot camp in recruiting, teaching me the basics of persuasion. In preparation, the company sent me a life-changing book called *How to Win Friends and Influence People* by Dale Carnegie. To this day, I still use the knowledge in that book.

My D-Day (discharge day) arrived, and I was off to Baltimore, Maryland for recruiter training. What a great concept: train the people the way you want them to operate before you send them into battle. Now this approach made sense to me. After all, I was the only candidate without a college degree selected in the entire class of 100. Not a single candidate in the room had served in the military. I had nothing in common with these young college kids. Talk about humility.

I made it through the boot camp and was assigned to the Glen Bernie, MD recruiting office. My 22-year-old boss immediately didn't like me. He was a frat house type guy, while I was a family man with responsibilities and no time for partying. Immediately, I knew I didn't belong. The shell-shock of trying to recruit people and the lack of respect the company's employees showed to temporary employees just saddened me. These temps were hard-working people, and they were treated just a little better than dirt. After two weeks in the recruiter business, I really hated my job. In my life, I had quit only one job. The first day I worked at a burger joint was the last day I worked at a burger joint. Now I had my first job out of the Marines, and I was going to quit with no backup offers on the table.

"Job One is a failure," I told my wife one evening. "There is no way I can survive there. My heart is not in it."

She was quiet and finally said, "If you're not happy, then quit."

So I did. Soon I was pounding on doors again. I really wanted to stay in the environmental field. I was zero for one in the civilian job world. I knew that hazardous material was where my heart was. If I didn't land a job soon, I would have to do what I had done before, work multiple jobs to pay the bills. My family needed the income. I was no stranger to Home Depot, Pep Boys, or grocery stores. I hoped that would not be the case. Our family could not survive on a single income.

About a month later, I received a call to interview for a large Fortune 500 construction company. I was going to accept the job, no matter what the pay for that type of work. Luckily, they were going to pay a little more than my Marine sergeant pay, with $14.00 an hour as the starting pay. If I'd learned anything from SSgt Fed, it was that no matter what the challenge was, I was going to succeed. I told myself that I would do whatever it took to be the best at what they assigned me. This opportunity was special. The company really wanted a college degree. I had to sell them on my credentials and specialized training. I needed to convince them that I was the right individual for the job. And I did. I couldn't let this opportunity pass me by.

On day one I showed up for work, and to my surprise, I was asked to meet with the president of the company. This company was a family business, and the president was one of three sons of the old man, as the employees affectionately called the founder of the company.

The president warmly invited me into his office. He had a strong New York accent and wore a white, long-sleeved shirt with his sleeves rolled up. His tie was neatly knotted. He was clean cut, with a serious look, a quiet smile, and graying hair. He introduced himself as Billy. I wasn't sure what to expect; I hadn't ever met a millionaire in real life. All I could think was: *Don't screw it up, Sean.*

Billy started off with some small talk and asked me what I thought of the company. I had done my homework and knew it was a family business. I knew the history of its founding in 1930. He liked that I was prepared, even though I didn't know the meeting was coming. He asked me about my military service.

"How can you tell that I was in the US military?" I asked.

It was the lack of much hair; I still had a regulation haircut. That style is something that just stays with you once you have been in for awhile.

He told me not to worry; he preferred clean-cut workers. Before we were through talking, he asked me one final question, "So what do you want to get out of working here?"

Without skipping a step, I told him that I wanted to learn enough to have his job.

He smiled back and said, "I believe that. You may just do that. I am going to watch you, and if you ever need anything, please let me know. Also, from now on, call me Billy instead of sir. I work for a living."

Finally, I thought, *a place I can fit in.*

In the end, there wasn't anything I wouldn't do for that guy. Billy earned my respect and admiration in a 15-minute meeting. I felt privileged. Afterwards, I was told that he made it a point to meet every new employee in his company.

Sean life lesson: do your homework about the company and the boss who hires you. I was employee number 700. The odds would be slim to meet the big boss in an organization that big. Even though I was sure I would never see the guy, I ended up meeting him right away, and my extra effort paid off. When I was called into the meeting, my preparation showed that I cared about the opportunity offered to me.

On a side note, when I interview people today, I always start with the question, "What do you know about my company?" Those people that have done their homework and can talk about the business almost always have a better interview with me. After all, everything you want to know about me or my firm is pretty much public and can be easily found online.

Once I started working for Billy, I was assigned to the environmental division. I was on the ground floor of the new Virginia environmental office. I was going to be mentored and led by a self-absorbed, chucklehead co-worker and my other boss, a professional geologist with absolutely no leadership skills. He talked to people like dirt. Guess what I was going to do? Make it work. What mattered the most was that I liked the company and the opportunity it would afford me. After all, we didn't get to pick our bosses in the Marines.

I had already committed myself to succeeding. The job entailed long hours and lots of road trips. My job was to represent the environmental department issues on all gas station construction projects involving environmental remediation in the Mid-Atlantic. I was part of a division responsible for dozens of gas station renovations. These gas stations needed to be cleaned and upgraded to comply with the Underground Storage Tank (UST) EPA laws. I spent my time in the field overseeing and performing environmental remediation and construction project activities.

I didn't know much about water treatment systems, pulling underground storage tanks, or all of the laws and rules governing them. Most of my environmental experience was in the Resource Conservation Recovery Act (RCRA) and the Clean Water Act (CWA), which were very different from the UST regulations. The good things going for me were that I knew how to work hard, and I knew how to ask questions.

More importantly, I knew how to learn. Thanks to the veteran construction superintendents (the sergeants) working in the field, I got a crash course. They all seemed to take a shine to me, probably because I did not treat them like my boss did and I wasn't arrogant like my coworkers. They wanted to help me because they knew I would bust my tail in the field, even it meant helping them with their jobs when my job was done. They also enjoyed working with a Marine.

These construction superintendents and I ended up working really well together. The company had so many construction crews out there that I had a chance to learn from a multitude of professionals. Those learning times were good for me. Sure, I made mistakes, but I learned that if I asked the right questions, I could prevent a vast majority of them. If I had learned anything at Job One, it was from Dale Carnegie. I practiced what he taught in his revered book like a religion. As he said, nobody likes a know it all. Humility and listening would be my key to success.

The great thing about life is that every now and then you get thrown a bone. You can eat it right there or you can save it for later and hope it will be there when you need it. The bone here at Billy's company was knowledge. For two and a half long years, I worked 60 to 80 hour weeks. I learned how to operate all manner of heavy equipment. I mastered pulling tanks out of the ground, and I learned how to be a team player in the unforgiving world of construction.

My final test came at an emergency oil spill response in Maryland. The Colonial pipeline broke near the Patapsco River in Maryland, losing over 330,000 gallons of number 6 bunker oil into the river. That oil is messy stuff. It sticks to everything. Guess what? The company needed a hazmat guru, and I was the only trained incident commander in the Virginia office.

Billy called me directly and told me to lead his team. With my knowledge and training, I would be the point man until backup arrived. The spill was so large that almost every spill response company on the East Coast had mobilized. Within days, companies from Alaska began arriving. The Patapsco River spill was a big one for an inland waterway.

For three days, I had a total of two hours of sleep. I was assigned hundreds of workers to start cleaning miles of beaches. The only problem was that Billy's client (I'll call him Ebenezer) would not let my team use the right tools and equipment for the job. Why? They were more expensive. Ebenezer in all his wisdom was trying to save money. He told us to use cheap, oil-absorbent tools that looked like cheerleader pom-poms to clean the spill up.

"Those things are useless!" I told him, while thousands of feet of effective absorbent boom sat in boxes in our fleet of trucks. "Let us use our equipment!" I implored.

It took Ebenezer a full day, but he finally allowed us to use the boom. Meanwhile, thousands of gallons of fuel oil floated down the river. More bad leadership! But I wasn't in charge; I wasn't Ebenezer.

If the Marines taught me anything, it was to use the tools you're trained to use. Unless you absolutely must, don't substitute good equipment.

At the same time, Ebenezer directed us to another beach to clean. He left me 200 hundred plant workers from the local power company - just abandoned all of us on this beach with no heavy equipment or trucks. Ebenezer thought it looked better to the governor, flying around in his helicopter, to see guys bent over in the river muck, picking up oil with pom-poms. It gave a much better impression, apparently.

What a joke.

The workers Ebenezer sent me had never cleaned a toilet bowl, from what I could tell. Their inexperience made the work ten times more dangerous and left me with a massive headache. To this day it still bothers me. It was the middle of winter, freezing cold, and every day the workers assigned to me made less and less progress. They'd clean the same beach 3 times because of Ebenezer's interference.

On the fourth day, Billy's company made one more common sense attempt to get supplies and resources to my beach. But Ebenezer denied us port-a-johns and instructed us to use the pom-poms when our supplies ran out. I made a decision. The workers were leaving.

I called Billy and told him what was going on. He said it was my call. I told him, "We are out of here!" I found the buses driving around dropping workers off at various sites. When I asked them to come pick up my team, they said no to me. In my polite Marine Corps way, I convinced them that either I could drive or they could drive, but one way or another the buses were going to take the men and women in my charge off the beaches. The drivers were eager to leave after that.

I felt that I passed my first civilian test that day. I proved that I could lead men and women into battle on the outside and survive. Fighting a large chemical spill is a battle, and we did it under some of the harshest conditions. It was a real milestone for a 26 year old.

But not long afterwards, near the end of 2000, the company fell on hard times. When I showed up to work in January 2001, the entire Virginia office was closed, and I was laid off. Little did I know that my life was going to change for the better.

Getting laid off might have been the best thing that ever happened to me. I mean that! While everyone was hugging each other and crying in the halls, I went to work on my resume.

During my two and half years with this construction company, I had managed and supervised environmental projects valued at over $68 million. I worked as a laborer, electrician, environmental technician, and equipment operator. I pulled wire, excavated dirt, demolished buildings, drilled monitoring wells, laid roofing shingles, and poured concrete pads and vaults. I installed thousands of feet of fitted pipe. I performed well and went from hazardous environmental technician to environmental foreman. Eventually, I became an incident commander for multiple hazardous materials spills for

Billy's company. I never turned down a project or backed away from a tough job. I applied everything I learned in the Marines about success. I gave the company all I had. In return, it gave me great opportunity and training.

Experience was the real key for me. Something my resume desperately needed was experience from the real world. Now, I could connect to the civilian workforce through my experience. The loss of the job did sadden me. Billy's company was full of really good people. I may have been just an employee, but the people in charge always knew my name. I would have worked for them as long as they would have had me. They knew that, too.

During my time with Billy's company, I used every opportunity to make connections, take business cards, and understand what made leaders tick outside of the military. I saw all of them as my mentors and examples of what I wanted to be and didn't want to be. I observed many good attributes, as well as flaws, in the people who worked with me.

I also paid attention to the discussions about our leaders from those on the bottom rung. I listened to the guys on the ground. They never seemed to understand. They were always bad-mouthing their bosses, never trying to understand that person's job or put themselves in that person's shoes. The critical attitude was systemic and new to me; I never saw it in the Marines. Sure, Marines grumbled and bemoaned our leadership from time to time, but we always followed our officers and got the job done.

I learned from these civilian workers that the higher up you get, the more you open yourself to attack. You are going to get criticized as a leader by the people who are not listening. That's why communication is so important. If your people understand your objective, they are more likely to get you there on time and on budget. Otherwise, they only hear what they want to hear. They make their work about themselves. If you're employed, try to put yourself in your boss's shoes and imagine what decision you would make.

Another *Sean life lesson: Do not personalize criticism. Learn from it and understand it.*

If the company had communicated better, being laid off would not have been such a blow. I knew that the business's cutbacks were not my fault. The owner had a decision: save 500 jobs or lose them all by not taking immediate action. My office just so happened to take the brunt of the employee reductions. From what I heard later in life, the company did everything it could to avoid the losses. It just had too much to handle without swift action.

After being laid off, I went back to the drawing board. The good news was that I had survived my first 3 years out of the Marines. The bad news was that I was unemployed again.

The layoff was a real setback for me. Up until then, I had never filed for unemployment. I can't remember not having a job. It seemed I had been employed most of my life, from snake catching to selling auto parts. That's why I felt this layoff was such a setback. I felt horrible going to the unemployment office; it was worse than leaving the Marines. But I needed the money. It was January, and work was slow. (Always try and be laid off in the spring if you can, especially if you're in construction. I say that in jest, but it's the truth. It was a cold winter, and I was unprepared.)

I was out of work four months. My wife was beside herself. She knew what my goals were, and she knew I wasn't getting there. I did what I could in the interim period. I took odd jobs and even drilled wells for a while. I had to stay in my field to be successful.

I wanted the excitement of doing chemical spill response again. Desperately, I wanted to see action. I applied to all of the top chemical response companies in the mid-Atlantic region. *This time is going to be different*, I thought. I was applying to be not just an employee but a manager. Equipped with my military experience and two and a half years in the field, I was going to be something special. All I had to do was to convince someone to hire me.

I got my big break later that year. One of the companies that had networked with me at the Patapsco River oil spill called me (I'll call them Responseco). Responseco wanted to offer me a position as the operations manager for the mid-Atlantic region. Their call marked a red-letter day for me; I was moving into management. After all, my plan was to go into chemical response and management.

I signed the offer letter for $50 thousand a year. The contract included a bonus for all sales I made and a half percent of the net based on the profitability of my region. Well, guess what? Responseco left one detail out: my region was losing $500 thousand a year! If I didn't turn the region around, the owner, a former Marine himself, was going to shut it down. I didn't mention that little tidbit to my wife. She would never have gone for such a risky deal. After all, she had never worked more than four stoplights from the house. Imagine that. What a gig!

I was working out of the Responseco Baltimore office but was assigned to Delaware City, Delaware. My first big job leadership-wise was acting as nighttime incident commander on a major chemical plant explosion. Nothing prepared me for this duty more than the Marines. Some 400 workers were searching around the clock for a union man who was killed during the explosion. A million gallons of sulfuric acid had been released from the tank explosion. With a PH between 0 and 2, the gas could kill you in minutes. The liquid could burn your skin in seconds.

The work was intensely dangerous. The lives and safety of the workers depended on me doing my job. I had no assistance, but I reveled in the opportunity. Just like that, at 28 years old, I was in charge of so many workers on such an important job! I'd never thought about it until now. It seemed natural then.

The only problem I had with Responseco was that I was greener than hell and it showed. The Marine in me wasn't so well received. I had a little too much get up and go, and I guess my personality rubbed a few people the wrong way. Politics was the watch word at the management level. Make the wrong enemies, and you would be through pretty quickly. I wasn't too sure Dale Carnegie's book had the answer to this one. I knew I had to work on that myself.

To help me get through these new challenges, I thought of how I struggled as a boy, transitioning from foster care to being an adopted son. I thought of how my mother made me find friends, riding my bike to the park. I knew I had to do that at my new assignment. Finding friends at Responseco was going to be harder than it looked. But now was the time to ride my bike to the park and find some friends in management, or this opportunity was going to be short-lived.

Luckily for me, I got a chance. My regional manager, John, was a salty, industrial guy from Pittsburgh. He was five feet six inches, balding, and had a mustache. With a bottle of Jack in hand and a cigarette out of his mouth, he was a real SOB. If he liked you, things were going to be okay. He was loyal. I could understand that. I didn't try to befriend him. In fact, I never wanted to be anything like him. But I did learn from him. And I believe he learned from me. We actually made a good team.

And guess what? He was in the same boat as I was. We both had to dig the worst-managed office out of the hole, or we were both going to be fired. Our relationship began with that common denominator. The thing I learned about making friends at the park was to find a common denominator. If you want to fire rockets with the other kids, you save your money and buy a rocket. (I did.) If you want to play football, take any position the other kids will give you. Don't ask to be quarterback. Earn the position, if that's what you want. You will make friends along the way.

I let John be the quarterback, and to keep my job I played any position from shovel technician to manager. Having a title didn't make you the boss. Once John figured out that Marines were loyal and reliable to a fault, he was glad to have me. He allowed me to grow and kicked my butt when I messed up (which I did a few times). John let me know how green I was, but he was still willing to work with me.

The setup at the new assignment was simple. Two full-time guys managed each office, and we relied on part-timers to do our work. We kept as many as 50 guys on call. Usually they were firefighters, paramedics, and other local workers who wanted to be trained in spill response.

John was a real cowboy. Once I learned that he wanted to conquer the world like the Macedonians in his ancestry, working with him somehow became fun. His only fault was not keeping receipts and tracking paper work. It drove me and corporate nuts. John and I both wanted to succeed, and we both bemoaned corporate and the lack of office support from Responseco. John was like Babe Ruth - once he got a project, he knocked it out of the ballpark! I learned how to perform the paperwork side of the management end, tracking the project costs and organizing the dollars, while performing midnight spill responses and being on call seven days a week. The great thing about being the operations manager was the word "manager." I worked on every spill call we received, literally hundreds of chemical calls, each with a unique challenge. There were rail car incidents, overturned tankers, gas leaks, and chemical spills of all shapes and sizes.

The call I remember the most occurred on September 11, 2001. It seemed the whole world blew up. The Twin Towers were attacked and on fire. The Pentagon was hit by another jet. And Flight 93 smashed into the ground near Shanksville, PA.

I was driving around Baltimore when our emergency pagers went off. We rushed back to the office just in time to see the second plane hit. The horror I felt inside told me immediately that what I saw was no accident. We were under attack. I wanted to call a recruiter and re-enlist on the spot, but the good Lord had another purpose for me. Besides, there was no way in hell that my wife would have let me reenlist.

But I was pissed off, and I wanted to do something. We had a contract with United Airlines. We were put on stand-by to support the Pentagon. The call never came, but it wasn't long before we were involved. In October, on top of all the fear and panic, someone decided to hit Congress with anthrax-laced letters.

When you're talking biological warfare, anthrax is a game changer. Responding to chemical spills is one thing. Responding to invisible biological organisms is completely different.

The call came in, and I was directed to Capitol Hill where I would speak directly with the captain in charge of the Capitol Hill Police bomb squad. My mission was simply to convince him that we could support his bomb squad with private sector responders to meet the urgent calls of white powder coming in from everywhere.

Talk about being nervous! I was the clean-cut jarhead that everyone (but myself) knew could sell the job. Well, I did just that. When I met the captain, I told him about Responseco and assured him that I would personally manage the project for him. I explained my Marine Corps background and shared my experience with him. Before I walked out that door, he told me that Responseco had the job and that we needed to get him a proposal ASAP. All of a sudden, our $500,000-in-the-hole office was saved. Not only were we saved, but we were going to bring more revenue into the company than the entire rest of the company combined.

Something changed that day. I discovered that I could sell a project, and not just any project, but one of those career-making projects. John worked up the bid, and I sold it to the customer. We offered time and materials indefinitely or until Responseco was not needed anymore.

The job started right away, and before too long the EPA noticed Responseco. The EPA was working on decontamination of the Hart Senate building. Senator Daschle's office had received a letter filled with anthrax, and a staffer opened it. So the whole building was being decontaminated.

With Christmas coming soon, most of the full-time employees of different contractors working on the project wanted to go home for the holidays. Their absence would severely impact the operation. When I heard the problem, I pitched the EPA on-scene coordinator. Ironically, we were able to connect from our mutual experience on the Patapsco River spill.

My performance there gave me a lot of credibility. Within 24 hours, Responseco had yet another contract in hand. Responseco was going to make millions of dollars from our office in a very few months.

Our office had grown so big that John and I had more personnel working for us than the entire rest of the company combined. Such significant growth really bothered the owner, whom I'll call Butch. Butch's arrogance showed when he would berate John and me over the phone about hiring people we needed. He wanted us to be beholden to his corporate administration team.

In my opinion, his administration team was not experiencing the fight we had to handle every day. I had to deal with the Centers for Disease Control (CDC), EPA, Capitol Police, private contractors, sub-contractors, prima donnas, and yahoos from every direction. In my opinion, Responseco's corporate was a bunch of desk commanders trying to dictate orders to the field about a situation they couldn't understand. If they wanted to lead, they should have visited the project. After all, something like this attack was new to everyone there. Only the military veterans understood the basics of nuclear, chemical, and biological warfare. People had lost their lives, and more could lose their lives if we weren't careful.

Sean life lesson: Get on the ground and see firsthand what's happening when possible. If you want to know what your people are doing and how they're doing it, join them.

But Butch trusted no one. He never came to the project site the entire time. Little did I know that this project was going to set a new path in motion for my career.

It wasn't long before the time for bonuses arrived. By my calculation, which was based on my signed hiring agreement with Responseco, I was owed $50,000. Not only did John and I turn Butch's losing office around, but we made him millions in profit. He had struck gold with his Baltimore office.

He sent me a bonus check of $300: $49,700 short of what I figured he owed me. This guy had just screwed me!

I had no time to deal with the injustice at the time. I had a job to do that needed everything I had, but I was not going to let this treachery go.

It's always amazing to me what happens when people get money in their pocket. They feel powerful. Money can create a false sense of security. You can see some people change for the worse, and you can also see some people change for the better.

Butch was off the planet. Soon after the new year, he struck, and the Baltimore Witch Hunt began.

Butch invited John to a public lunch. There he accused John of stealing. Instead of thanking and rewarding my mentor and boss, Butch fired him. I said to myself: *Hmm, I guess I am next!* John warned me of what was coming as he packed and left. Stunned, I had no reason to doubt him. Responseco was launching a coup of our office.

I could see the writing on the wall. Butch didn't want to pay his contract bonus, because it would have been near six figures. I for one was not going to be hung out to dry. Corporate wanted me to write a letter saying that John stole from the company. He never stole a nickel, because I kept the books and the job records. I refused to write the letter. Corporate intended to discredit John by trashing him in front of the other employees. What would they do to me? I knew my job was at stake. I also knew that when I confronted Butch about the bonus, he would fire me, too.

I waited a bit, but eventually I traveled to headquarters in New Jersey to confront Butch, my fellow Marine. When I got there, the office personnel didn't even know who I was. I introduced myself and asked to speak to Butch. He met me in his office. I was armed with my signed offer letter wherein Responseco had agreed to pay me half a percent of the profit I and my office made.

"Butch," I said. "Why did you send me $300 for my bonus? You owe me $50,000. That was our agreement. That was your word and your bond."

He looked at me, as some arrogant fools with money will do, and began to tell me how important I was to the firm. But then he said that I was still young and naïve. He said he could teach me.

I listened, and after he was done pontificating on how wonderful he was, I asked him again, "Butch, why didn't you pay me what you owed me for my services?"

He responded sharply. "I changed the company handbook. Operations managers are no longer entitled to bonuses. That change supersedes your agreement." Then he really poured it on thick! "You know, I have the ability to make good things happen for you."

"You're right!" I said. "Now please make good on your agreement. Pay me what was agreed, then we can talk about other good things."

"That's not going to happen!" Butch said. "But here is what I will do. I will give you a $15,000 a year pay increase right now." He wrote out a check for $15,000 with my name on it.

Thinking back, maybe I should have taken it. I didn't, though. "You can keep it. You will have my resignation on your desk in the morning!"

His parting words to me were even funnier. He said, "You are nothing without me!"

As I drove down the road away from his office, knowing that I had just quit what I thought would be my dream job, I was shattered and disillusioned. How was I going to explain this news to my wife? "Great news! We have no income again."

To make matters worse, Butch's vice president called to fire me while I was on the way home, even though I had resigned. He was a heartless bastard, too. They served each other well.

Now I was fed up with the civilian job market. I loved the work I did, but I hated the fact that people with more power and responsibility than I had were controlling my destiny. Now was the time for me to dream bigger than big. I was going to open my own business, one that would rival the others. I just wasn't sure exactly how I was going to do it.

I was twenty-nine and jobless with just $1,600 bucks to my name, but I promised myself one thing. I would do it!

First, I was going to help close down Butch and Responseco. He was going to understand what he'd had and what he could have had. It took me six months, but I contacted every client that I had brought in and moved them to other companies. In the process, John sued Responseco for wrongful termination. I knew that he and I would meet again. Until then, though, I had to focus on starting my own business.

I guess you could accuse me of being a dreamer. I dreamt of being successful all of my life. I dreamt of finding my biological family. I dreamt of many things, and now I was going to act. I was the guy who imagined that I could save the world, change lives, and do something magnificent. Just maybe somebody would see me and recognize me for my efforts.

Making that long drive back to Virginia from New Jersey, I knew that the future without a safety net would be difficult. But I remember feeling a sense of freedom, maybe even a sense of relief, as I drove.

Yes, I'd just resigned my job. Yes, I had no backup job. I had to be responsible for myself from now on. After what seemed like an eternity of challenging leaders and bosses, I had my own success in my hands. I was going to have to work my butt off if I wanted to succeed. I knew from my past that I had the instinct and work ethic to survive. The two real questions before me were simple: Could I lead myself? And could I lead others in my own organization?

I had very little experience in managing a business and none in starting one, but I felt compelled to try. To answer those two questions would take a while. I was employee number one, and the first thing I had to do was convince my wife that my plan was not insane. Opening a business would be a good thing. I was young, and if I fell down, I knew I could get back up. There would be other opportunities.

My wife was the conservative side of reason. The thought of me going self-employed terrified her. But she gave me her blessing with the caveat that if it didn't go well, I had to be ready to flip some burgers.

Sean life lesson: Just because it's there for the taking doesn't mean you have to take it. Someone who wrongs you in business will most likely do it again and construe your acceptance as forgiveness. My ex-employer wasn't entitled to the opportunity to mistreat me again.

Chapter 4:

Charting a New Course

Sean P. Jensen

AT the same time that my business life was transitioning, my personal life was taking a positive turn. Although I was still estranged from my adopted family, I was making progress. Early in 2000, I had made a major discovery. Coming home from work one day, I received a large manila envelope containing old personal records (pre-adoption). Claudette was in the process of cleaning out old files and documents like school records and sending them to her kids. Her reorganization opened the door for me to discover who I was. Being in foster care was very painful to me. And the lack of knowing who I was and where I came from troubled me for a long time. The older I got, the more I was getting over these issues, but I still wanted to close that loop someday. To move past that portion of my life would not only clear my head, but it would also be the key for me to focus on the future.

I stood in my kitchen in utter amazement, poring over the photos, records, old report cards, and vital information the state had kept. I didn't know that Larry and Claudette had these records. When the state turned them over to my adopted parents, no one said anything to me.

Life has a funny way of changing the rules. Sometimes what happens may seem cruel, but I personally believe that everything happens for a reason. I am a staunch believer in destiny.

So when I found my school medical records from New York, I was stunned to see two names: Amelia and Richard were listed as my biological parents. They were real! I had found a critical clue to my past. Faded from 24 years in storage, there was an address. I was able to pinpoint the house where I lived before moving to Florida. Now I just had to find the owner.

I knew in my heart that it would be just a matter of time before I could speak to my biological family again. Technology was moving faster and faster in the 1990s, and by the year 2000, finding information was pretty much a matter of pointing and clicking. With a little work, I would find the owners of my former home quickly. I could tell that the current owners of the house on record had been the same for many years. Did they know my parents? Did they have an old lease? Would they have the answers about my adoption that I'd been wondering nearly all my life?

Finding the owners of the property took me about two weeks. Sadly, the owners lived in New Jersey. Because their house had been owned for many years, I immediately thought it was a rental property. I was able to track down the phone number of the owners, and I called them. But the lady answering the phone kept stalling me. She must have thought I was telemarketer.

I kept asking for Paul and Elizabeth, who did not have the same last name of either of my parents. I tried explaining to her that I was related to the family that lived in the house in the early 70s and that it was critical I talk to Paul or Elizabeth. She told me that Paul would get back to me. I explained to her that if I didn't speak to Paul or Elizabeth I would be coming up. After that final conversation, I received the phone call that changed my life.

I was working at Andrews Air Force Base at the time under a temporary contract, and the call came around lunchtime. Paul was on the phone. He immediately started asking a lot of questions. I had more than he did. He was guarded, as if he knew something strange was up. We started going back and forth.

"Paul," I asked. "Has the house been in your family for a long time?"

"Yes," he replied.

"Sir, are you the original owner of record?" I asked.

He replied, "The house has been in my family a long time."

Getting excited, I pressed, "Do you have renters there, or would you have names of previous tenants?"

He said he had information.

Almost dancing with the excitement of my questions, I then asked if he knew who lived in the house in the years 1970-1976. And he did. Getting concerned about all of my questions, Paul then asked me who I was and why I had all these questions. He must have sensed something.

I told him directly that I was adopted and that my siblings and I lived in that house in the early seventies. I told him that it was vital for me to try to locate him because I wanted to learn more about myself. I had been searching a very long time, and I was hoping to find my family. Then I asked him if he knew who Amelia was, and he said, "Yes."

There was a slight pause and an audible sigh on the other end of the phone. I couldn't imagine what would happen next.

"Sean," he quietly said, "I am your grandfather, Paul. Your mother, Amelia, is my daughter. You have found us!"

I fell to my knees weak from the excitement of this discovery.

I couldn't believe it. All these years searching in libraries and cold- calling people with my last name at birth, I had discovered no clues. Then everything I needed just showed up one day in a manila envelope. This critical discovery opened doors I had never imagined. Then I wondered: *Will they talk to me? Will they remember me?*

My grandfather told me that he would have to notify my mom that I had found him and ask her if she wanted to talk with me. I already knew that my biological mother might not want to speak to the son she left behind. I believed that she would call me, but I couldn't be certain. I had played out all the scenarios in my head time and time again. I thought of how I would scope my family out first and see if I wanted to meet them or if it seemed like they wanted to meet me. It had been 20 years! I wondered if they would be weird. Would they be a crime family? Who knew? It didn't matter now.

I went home that night with tears of joy. I told my wife what had happened. It was so surreal. Finding my family would be my turning point. I told myself that I would forgive them, no matter what, and move on. This meeting would be my opportunity. About a week passed, during which my whole house was on phone watch. Finally, one night the phone rang, and my daughter answered it. The phone call was for me.

I picked up the phone and said, "Hello."

"Hello, son, it's your mom, Amelia."

You could have knocked me over with a feather. It was my biological mother!

You see, when I was very young I learned a valuable lesson about perseverance. I never gave up the search. I took a break from time to time, but I never gave up looking for my family. The *Sean life lesson: Sometimes the path to success will lead you through many pitfalls.* If you quit, you will never find success. Sometimes there is a plan you cannot control, and sometimes getting the answers you want takes two decades. Never quit.

Amelia and I spoke for three hours that night. Mostly we talked about my past and the distant memories she could confirm, like the bullies I beat up when I was five years old. (My mom had made me apologize to them and their parents, even though they were picking on me.) I was reconnecting with myself at the same time that I was reconnecting with her. While I recalled these times from my past, I realized how happy I was as a young boy, before my life was flipped upside down.

Soon after this call, my grandfather, his wife, and my mother came to Virginia to meet me and my little sister. I picked him up at the train station and my mother at the airport. My grandfather never forgot me. He had a picture of me in his wallet when we met. He had carried me for 20 years! Our reunion was an extraordinary event, considering how much time had passed. For the first time in decades, I felt truly whole again. Now I could finally move on and close the circle that had haunted my thoughts for so long. This significant mystery had been solved.

This event also contributed to me starting a business. I figured that if I could find my biological family, like a needle in a haystack, I could do anything! Providentially, I learned during our meeting that I was Hawaiian and Greek. This information about me would have a major impact in my business future. I also found out that my father had passed away, as well as my grandparents on both sides, except Grandpa Paul. Nevertheless, I was able to connect and learn about my history.

Hawaiian culture and my identity as a Hawaiian provided me a sense of relief, not only because of my sense of belonging, but also because it gave me a perspective on things that were already true of me. I knew that family was of paramount importance to me. Just look at my demands for my siblings as a young child and my persistent search for my birth family.

Now I had a name for that importance: ohana. And I knew that I was strong and determined already. Now I knew that I was part of a strong and determined people. And I knew that I was patient and calm, but now I saw that patience and calm tied to a people that learned their patience and calm from living between the tempestuous sea and unforgiving volcanoes. Embracing my Hawaiian family allowed me to embrace myself in a way that I had never done before.

I never directly asked what happened when I was six. There were, of course, several sides to the story volunteered by my mother and grandfather as to how we ended up where we did. I also had the info that Claudette told me as well. In this case, I politely told my family that I was okay with the past and that we would move forward from where we were and make the best of our newfound relationship. I had spent countless restless nights not being able to sleep, just wondering about my personal history. At last, I could let go of the past and strive for a better future. While I was sleeping that night, my wife had to check me, because I was so quiet that she thought I was dead.

All the family history led to my pulling into my Virginia driveway after the trip back from New Jersey to confront Butch. Meeting my biological mother

58

in 2000 had given me a sense of empowerment. My life had come full circle. I told myself that I could do anything. I was ready to be an entrepreneur. But first, I would need to explain it to my wife.

I entered the house and slowly explained the day's events. My wife was disappointed that we were going to be without a salary again. She reminded me that I had a good job that was paying the bills. She cautioned me that we would struggle like before if my new venture didn't work. We were finally getting on track from the hard time we had after I was laid off from Billy's company. We could not afford for me to be out of work for long. This was not a good time for me to screw up. Nicole peppered me with questions: "Who is going to do your accounting? How are you going to make payroll for yourself? How will you start a business with only $1,600?"

I told her of my consultant plan. I would start calling everyone I knew. I'd waste no time. My approach was going to be fairly straightforward. I would resell all of the contracts I landed at Responseco and start a hazmat company with a new firm. As luck would have it, there was a small environmental industrial maintenance firm in Baltimore that needed me. They just didn't know it yet.

Sean P. Jensen

Part Two-

Polu Kai

Blue Ocean

Sean P. Jensen

Chapter 5:

Captain of My Own Ship

Sean P. Jensen

I never doubted myself, not one bit. The previous few years of my life had been a growing period. I made the scary transition from being US Marine to a civilian. I went from technician to operations manager to salesman. I found my biological family. I sold my first contract of what would be hundreds of millions of dollars' worth of contracts in my life. I worked on projects of incredible importance to my career. I built a personal resume that stood on its own this time.

Through all of these experiences, I had discovered that I could do anything I set my mind to by listening, watching, and learning. I had steered other captains' ships safe to shore, and now it was time for me to steer my own. Things were going to be fine. All I had to do is was create the opportunities.

You wouldn't believe how easy it was to get a business license. I drove down to the Fairfax, Virginia government center; completed a one-page application, applying under environmental consulting; paid $25; and I was totally legal. Just like that, on April 13, 2002, I was a sole proprietor duly recognized by Fairfax County, Virginia. I started as a consultant before that date, but that's the day I went official.

You may want to laugh, but I thought my new company was a big deal. My title was the same as John D. Rockefeller. I was president and chief executive officer of Charlotte's Consulting. (The name of my company came from my daughter Charlotte. That's what happens when you ask your 11 year old for help naming your company.)

I worked the phones extensively. I let everyone know that I was starting a business and that I was available to work. I had saved every business card and every contact for a reason: You just don't know when you will actually need them.

Working the phones and having the business contacts paid off quickly. I landed a day job setting up hazardous material disposal teams and selling environmental work for a small industrial maintenance firm in Baltimore, Maryland - the one I mentioned earlier. I'll call them SIMC.

The drive was grueling every day, but I needed to have a steady source of income. SIMC gave me a consulting salary of $6,000 a month, and I gave them 100% of my effort. We had a good relationship. I sold over a million dollars in contracts for them until I could get my business moving along.

They supported me as a consultant and even wanted to buy into the firm.

I worked my butt off for SIMC. All day, I devoted every ounce of effort to my job, and at the end of the day, I was still on call.

When I was not working for SIMC, I focused on building my own business. In preparation for an anticipated increase in work, I began the paperwork to incorporate Charlotte's Consulting as an LLC. It was the easiest type of corporation to incorporate because you could be a sole member LLC.

One day, I was overseeing a large underground storage tank removal project near Capitol Hill. Sitting in my work truck during a blizzard, I was chatting with a subcontractor named Harry who was working on the project with me. While chattering on how freezing cold it was outside, he asked me where I got my tan. I laughed and told him I had just returned from visiting my mother in Hawaii. He asked me if I was Hawaiian, and I confirmed that I was. His eyes lit up as I told him my life story.

Harry was especially interested in how I learned that I was native Hawaiian. You see, as a native Hawaiian I was eligible to participate in a unique Small Business Administration (SBA) program called the 8(a) program. Harry explained the program to me and what it was capable of doing for a young entrepreneur. He convinced me that I had to explore it myself. What I found online was nothing short of a miracle. It really was a program that could help a young entrepreneur like me.

Soon after that discussion with Harry, I decided to apply for the 8(a) program. The minimum requirements were pretty straightforward. It seemed everything I had been doing in my life was getting prepared for this moment. I just needed to follow the instructions.

My personal net worth had to be less than $250,000 (check). I had to prove I was a native Hawaiian, and my family had to be indigenous to the Hawaiian Islands prior to 1775. That was easy now that I had found my biological mother. She was born in the Territory of Hawaii, and my deceased grandmother and several grandparents were all native Hawaiians.

Our lineage went straight back to the to the Kingdom of Hawaii. Having the genealogy done and finding my biological mother was critical, or I would never have been allowed into the program. Thank the Lord, I didn't have to go back to 1775!

I also needed two years in business or a spectacular resume showing leadership and business management experience to get a waiver. Well, I had a great resume that included some major recognizable projects. I also had to prepare a business plan that would show the potential for success.

Writing this plan proved a bit more difficult, but it was nothing I couldn't overcome. The only other problem was the fact that my company only had one employee: myself. I enlisted the help of an 8(a) application consultant, and with the money I had been saving, I was able to have someone review my SBA application. The package was long and tedious.

Sean life lesson: If you can afford to have a professional look over your work, a second opinion is always helpful.

In August 2003 I finished incorporating my company and decided that things were going to be different. I changed the name of the company to Polu Kai Services, LLC, first because I saw the need to incorporate my Hawaiian lineage. Second, if you're going to be unique, why not go big? "Polu Kai" in Hawaiian means "blue water," and my favorite thing of all is the ocean. I love the ocean. After a lengthy thought process, I settled on "Services" because I knew I could cast a wider net with that description. I wouldn't be boxed in by using such words as "construction" or "environmental" in the company title. Using "services" instead allowed me to cross the gamut of work.

I'm always intrigued with people who name their businesses after themselves. I could not imagine being Jensen LLC or S. Jensen Incorporated. If you fail, your name might as well be mud. If you fail with your name on the business, you're looking at career quicksand, and you might as well hang it up. I didn't want to risk my name. I knew that everyone would botch up saying the corporate name, but I also knew that they would remember it. There were so few SBA-certified native Hawaiian companies in the world. I could only find 4 SBA-registered native Hawaiian firms in the government marketplace at the time. This was going to be fun.

At this time, I was still doing consulting for SIMC. Preparing to enter the 8(a) program, I sent the package application in and waited. During that time, I got a really nice opportunity from a friend of a friend of a friend down at the defense depot in Richmond. I had been waiting for an opening like this. There was a task to do, an environmental survey and some repackaging of hazardous materials. I fired off a quote for $13,000. The client accepted my offer. And like that, I had my first project where I could keep everything I earned.

The only issue I had with SIMC was that the leadership wanted me to sell my business for them and work for SIMC exclusively. I knew that I had to cut ties. SIMC had been good to me, but it was not going to let me earn my own revenue. I had to start my company on my own. There was a heated discussion between me and the owner of SIMC, who accused me of selling work on his time. The charge wasn't true. SIMC just wanted the revenue for my first project to be coming into them.

But their charge was a problem with ethics for me. To be truthful, I gave much more than 40 hours a week to SIMC, and I couldn't do their consulting and work for Polu Kai at the same time. I severed ties with SIMC. Now I was all in. If I screwed this company up, I really had no plan; burger flipper was probably next on the list for me. I remembered the unemployment line and marched out to control my own destiny.

My first day on the project, I drove my beat-up Ford Explorer to Richmond. This $13,000 fee was a big deal. Since most of it was labor, I had a real honey of a project. The client came out to meet me and asked me for a business card. He looked at me and said, "I don't usually meet the presidents of the companies we use. In particular I don't see guys like you holding a ladder at the job site." I quickly let him know that what he needed was a small job and that I would have it done in no time. I didn't get what he said until later in life. He must have thought he hired one guy and a pickup truck. Well, he did.

One thing I know about people is that many have been given the opportunity to grow and succeed, but they are just not smart enough or emotionally perceptive to see it. I had vision, though. I was going to use this project as a stepping stone to success.

Working on the project was lots of fun. I didn't mind the 14-hour days, including the 4 hours a day I spent driving back and forth to Richmond. This time, the money was coming into my pocket. Having my first real job working for myself was great. I was in my element back on a military base. I was going to break out of the consulting world and hopefully hire my first employees.

Life is about creating opportunity, and when you do get the opportunity you have to recognize it, rise up, and seize the moment. Soon a colonel, the commander of an Air Force base, would give me an opportunity.

One day, he stopped by to chat with me. He was telling me how the Virginia Department of Environmental Quality was giving him a hard time. He couldn't figure out why no one in his organization had answers for him, and he wondered how to get the state off his back on chemical storage issues.

I told him what I did for Quantico as a sergeant in the Marines. I explained my role there and how I handled federal and state regulators on a daily basis. I told him that his warehouses were going to blow up because they had incompatible chemicals next to each other.

I also explained to him how the chemicals would react if they didn't make changes. I told the good colonel that he was going to have to set up an inspection process and correct those deficiencies to get the state off of his back.

He asked me what I would do. I gave him my solutions, which involved repackaging materials, doing a full-blown analysis of their stored materials, and making some simple changes to his storage layout and set up. Normally, you don't talk with another company's clients without permission; that courtesy is good form and shows respect for your customer.

To me, I thought I was engaging in harmless small talk. I was just giving some free advice; I didn't ask for anything. As I finished the discussion with the colonel, I wished him good luck. He told me thanks for the advice and asked me who I was working for. I gave him the name of my first clients, Micropact Engineering.

Before too long, my client was calling me up. Our talk went something like this: "Hello, Mr. Jensen - you wouldn't have had a conversation with a certain full-bird colonel the other day, would you? He said something to us about a Marine sergeant.

I replied that I did and then I proceeded to explain what I'd told the colonel.

My client paused and asked, "Did you know that he commands the base?" I didn't.

At the time, I was unaware of his title or position. All I knew was that he was a colonel in the Air Force.

That's when my client asked me point blank the following question: "Can you please provide me a technical price proposal for all of the things you told him? He wants you to do the work personally."

My heart jumped inside. I knew this was a big project.

You know what they say, "If you talk the talk, you had better walk the walk."

I did just that. I put my proposal together as instructed. Afterwards, I was worried about the dollar figures. It was over $330,000. Most of the cost was my labor, but I had to hire a subcontractor. I also had to get additional insurance. Would this bid even work? Hell, if the client put me through the wringer on $13,000, how would they react to $330,000?

I sent the proposal in. My client dutifully marked up my numbers to present to the government. I did not get an immediate reaction. As I waited each day to get the news, I worried more. Silence was the worst! I didn't know if I was wrong or right on the numbers, and I wouldn't until I got the call. In my case, I was right. My subcontract was modified up from $13,000 to $330,000! That was more money than I had personally earned in the last four years of my life combined. I would make that figure in five months.

The project went well. I even got to enlist a former colleague of mine as a sub-consultant. I found that the security you feel when you have a backlog of work and the joy you get from completing a great project are indescribable. This work would pay the bills. It also helped augment the pay I was getting, which was $3,000 a month. I put the majority back into the business and paid my taxes.

I had very simple goals in business: Pay your employees, pay your taxes, and pay yourself. In order to do so, you have to have more money coming in than going out. That basic rule is one that I have followed. While it sounds simple, you must be disciplined in the handling of the money you earn. If you're running a business, you don't take money for yourself just because it's there. You will spend it, and you will have a very short business life. It does take money to make money. You have to be somewhat secure to take risks. I tried to have six months' of salary in the bank at all times. I had to stretch it if I was going to make it. I knew that the next jobs would not be so easy. $3,000 a month was what my wife had agreed to expect for her house budget. I had to deliver that amount without fail.

January 2004 brought new opportunities. After I paid my bills and my taxes, I had nearly eight months of pay from the work performed in 2003. I had a whopping $24,000 in the bank after paying all of my startup costs in full, including accountants, consultants, credit cards, etc. In reality, I was able to go debt free and have a cash reserve within the first year and a half of the business. To the average guy, those numbers would sound good, but I was still shortchanging myself with my monthly salary. After all, I had been making $6,000 a month from SIMC before I decided to go out on my own.

Thank the Lord, my wife was holding her own in the banking business at the same time. I kept telling her that I would strike it big. She would give me her skeptical smile, probably just waiting for me to say, "Hey, I am going to hang it up." At the time, maybe she thought that this business idea was just a mid-life crisis or something and that I would go get a regular job soon. However, my luck suddenly changed for the better when I received notice from the SBA that I was approved to enter the 8(a) program. I received the waiver in business, and I was approved as a Native American-owned business with the added addition of now being native Hawaiian-owned.

I don't think that the SBA knew where to classify me. Native Hawaiian-owned was at the time a relatively new addition to the 8(a) program. I believe that I was one of the first companies certified by SBA on the east coast, not based in Hawaii, to get into the program with that designation. Applying had been quite a challenge, and I was so happy to have the paperwork that I really didn't care where the SBA put me. I had really done my homework, and I knew that the 8(a) program would be helpful to my success. I didn't know how important; I just knew it was key.

The only issue I had with Polu Kai Services (PKS) was that it was still just me. During that time, I set out on a journey of marketing and business development. I worked the phones constantly, and I got a few bites here and there. But PKS still really wasn't moving in the direction I hoped.

At one point in the spring of 2004, I landed a nice project at Ft. Monroe with my old friend John from Responseco. His new company was a prime contractor on a demolition project, and he needed an asbestos consultant. Through my network of business contacts, I found the right consultant for him. I put a proposal together for him, and he awarded me a contract. The guy I hired as a consultant had just gone through a bad divorce, and believe it or not, he was in a worse financial position than I was. He couldn't afford the lodging to work at the site; so he begged me for an advance until the money came in. All in all, it was a $30,000 project. PKS stood to make $10,000. Ten grand is big money when you are one guy and a pickup truck. In my mind, I'd extended the life of my company by three more months.

The consultant I hired seemed like a true Christian. He called himself one. He promised me the world, and he did great for the first three months. As the project was getting ready to move to the second phase, the good Christian turned out to be a wolf in sheep's clothing. He stabbed me in the back. Unbeknownst to John or me, he had convinced the project manager that he could do the job cheaper and better than me. He stole the work for himself. Business mimics life, and I learned that no good deed goes unpunished. Unfortunately for me, I really didn't have a lot cooking, and I could see the writing on the wall. No work meant out of business. I tried to keep this setback quiet with my wife, but she knew I was struggling.

Could I continue? Could I really pull this venture off? I contacted John. He told me that the decision was out of his hands. The company wanted the extra money the Christian promised them in savings, and though the owner knew about the issue, he would do nothing to act. Frustrated, I moved on. The long, hot summer of 2004 was moving along, and it would take the Cape Verde Islands to save me.

Little did we know at the time that the summer of 2004 was the beginning of one of the wildest hurricane seasons in modern history. Since I had grown up in Florida, I knew the power of these storms. What I didn't know was that the Federal Emergency Management Agency (FEMA), the primary response agency for these disasters, did not work alone.

The US Army Corps of Engineers (USACE) had a very strong disaster relief mission, including delivering emergency power, debris removal, and temporary roofing. Roofing was usually necessary during disaster responses in the Caribbean, due to the poor construction of roofs and the very high winds. The same thing happened in Florida. The sheer magnitude of the destruction overwhelmed the homeowners and insurance adjusters. In order to protect the leaking roofs and damaged properties, someone would have to act, and those people would be FEMA and the USACE. While I knew everything anyone needed to know to respond to a major chemical or biological incident, I knew very little about natural disaster responses.
Shortly after I lost the asbestos gig, a storm hit, and my friend John called me up.

"Sean, are you going to Florida?" he asked.

I said, "No. What would I do there?"

"Blue-roof!" he replied. "Anyone can nail plastic to a roof - even you."

I paused a minute and then replied, "John, I have never done anything like that."

He laughed me off like he always did. "Sean, think of it as a chemical spill! All you need is a contract and some plastic. You'll be fine. If you can run 400 people cleaning up oil, you can run 400 people putting tarp on a roof."

Before he hung up, he told me to call him back when I got a contract. I immediately got on the USACE website and started dialing prime contract holders. There were six prime contract holders that would all need subcontractors. As I went down the list, the response got worse and worse. Most did not want to talk to me, and many didn't even pick up the phone.

Then I came upon a guy named Dave who was located in Dothan, Alabama. His company was a prime contractor and also an 8(a) like me. He asked me if I was a roofer. I was honest and told him I wasn't but that I was hungry and wanted the work. I didn't want to lie to get the job. He had a long Alabama drawl, and I knew I was dealing with a real player here. I was worried. If he hung up on me, would that be the end of Polu Kai?

"Well," he began again in his slow Southern accent, "what do you do?"

I told him that I could manage any chemical or biological disaster he could throw at me. More importantly, I explained that I could lead and manage hundreds of personnel under extreme pressure.

He paused for another second. "Send me an email. You are number three on the list to mobilize to Punta Gorda."

My heart stopped for a minute as I said to myself: *John was right! Now I have to figure out where I am going to find an army to do this work.*

I called John back and told him the score. He informed me that his company wouldn't support me because disaster response was not something they did. Then he told me the real reason was that the owner was scared and didn't want to work with a one-person firm. Who would subcontract to me and go on this daring mission to make a million dollars? I knew there had to be that much there, because the contract values exceeded $50 million on all six contracts.

Remember what I said about networking and keeping every card you ever receive? There is a lot of good in that habit. After talking to numerous companies, I was able to reach a firm in Baltimore, another 8(a), and convince them to join the team. They were an environmental firm. The most important thing they had was cash. I had never worked with them before, but I was desperate. I really had to believe in myself now, more than ever.

Just before we were to mobilize to Punta Gorda, the phone rang. It was Dave. We all had been watching Hurricane Ivan moving through the Caribbean. Forming off the Cape Verde Islands, it had crossed the Atlantic and was becoming a monster. Everyone knew that Ivan was going to be a powerful hurricane causing major damage.

Dave asked that I stand by and be prepared to mobilize anywhere he directed within 24 hours. I knew then that I wasn't necessarily going to Punta Gorda anymore. I called Tom, my new strategic teaming partner in Baltimore, and broke the news. During the conversation I had with Dave, he also went over the insurance requirements needed to work for his company. I didn't meet those requirements. What was I going to do? I had sold myself as a prime subcontractor, but I didn't have the money or the experience to get workman's comp, auto, or general liability insurance. As an established company, Tom had that money and experience. There wouldn't be any time for me to get insurance set up. I had to make a strategic decision, the first of many.

I knew I had to give up the prime subcontractor role and let Tom's company take it. The good thing about our relationship was that we needed each other. Something you have to know in business is that for two parties to work together, each has to have a common objective where both entities bring commensurate value. Tom recognized the value of the contract, my relationship with the prime contractor, and the potential money that could be earned. I had the experience he needed to run the job and make it successful. In some ways, this job would be like old times. I needed the support and infrastructure to back my sales pitch, just like I had in my previous relationships. Success or failure depended on my leadership and my ability to take a back seat. I was willing to do that here to make my mark.

Soon we worked out the particulars. I would get 20% of gross, and Tom would fund the project and provide me with people. All I had to do was ensure that he got the contract. We drafted a simple teaming arrangement in fair terms. The next thing I had to do was to convince Dave to buy into Tom. I made the call and convinced Dave that Tom and I would not fail. I would run the show, and Tom would be the prime subcontractor.

Then Hurricane Ivan hit. The devastation was complete from Orange Beach, Alabama to Santa Rosa County, Florida. Ivan downgraded to a category 3 storm as it hit, but it still did immense damage. I got a call from Dave, who directed me to Pensacola, Florida. He told me that he had almost all of Escambia County, the strike zone for this wicked storm. He said that the work was first come, first served.

I had $6,000 in the bank at the time and another $4,000 in available credit. I kissed my wife goodbye and told her I would be back soon. This job wasn't the first time I'd left home. This time was different, though. I would come home either a hero or a zero.

Nothing can prepare you for the enormity of the destruction I witnessed. The best way to describe my arrival in Pensacola was that it was like driving through a recently bombed-out city. It looked as if a B-52 strike had happened the night before. As the daylight from the sunrise arrived, my view of the destruction became clear as day. I had been all over the world and seen my share of dilapidation and poverty. Hurricane Ivan had pushed Pensacola back into the Stone Age. Nothing was functioning except the National Guard and the local police. With no equipment and flying by the seat of my pants, I found a vacant shopping mall. In it, there was ample space to set up an operation along a main highway. Having never supervised this kind of work before, I figured we would need to set up a camp; at least, that's what my Marine experience told me.

I located Dave the following day. I shook hands with him, and he handed me a map. "Welcome to Pensacola. Where would you like to work?" Having done a bit of recon the day before, I knew the damage would be worse close to shore; so I took us inland a few miles, circled the area, and said that we would take it. I hoped that the wind would have de-shingled more houses than it destroyed. I knew that the work would be easier for us that way. Truth be told, most of our area was in an older section of town where many of the roofs were original to the construction of the houses. I had brought Ken and Grant with me. They were old-timers in the business. One handled the administration, and the other would handle the men. Now all I needed were Tom's workers.

When you are trying to be successful in the emergency response business, you get used to working with temporary workers. They complain about how little they make. They complain about the work. Yet, if you treat them right, they manage to get you to the end of a project. If you spoil them, they see you as weak. If you work with them, they see you as strong. At the end of the day, a majority of the temporary workers I am talking about will drink their paychecks away before payday. Tom's workforce was that bunch. The first night they got to Pensacola, they immediately set upon me complaining that this wasn't what they signed up for. Man, was I in for a ride!

One individual, a self-declared leader of the bunch, approached me. He was a big tall brother named Darryl who informed me that he had just been released from jail. Darryl told me that he was also an ordained minister. Smiling, I told Darryl that I appreciated his religious convictions and that it was all right for them to have church on Sundays. Then I asked if he would be leading the service. He said he would. I told him that was great and that we would have his sermon at 5AM. After that, we would all go to work. He looked at me and uttered, "Say, what?"

I told Darryl that Jesus wanted him working and that the good people of Pensacola needed his help. I also reminded him that this was a free country and that he was free not to have a job if he didn't work. Darryl had made the first move. I knew I would be playing games like this every day for as long as it took to accomplish the mission.

Cell phone service was spotty, but I managed to keep in touch with home. The crew and I finally got to work, and the jobs kept coming. Under my leadership, we blue-tarped over 2000 houses in 45 days. By Thanksgiving, I was coming home with $200,000 in my pocket. Polu Kai was saved again!

Darryl did not make it through the whole project. He came back to the camp high on PCP one day and almost killed me and some other workers. We managed to get the police there in time to take him to jail. It was a real shame. Another guy named Grant ended up getting hooked on drugs and had to get out of town before the dealers found him. A worker named Ken managed to stick it out till the end. Of course, I had to pay both Ken and Grant a share of what I made on my deal. After all, they didn't come down to Florida for their health; they came down to get paid. Tom ended up sticking me for $18,000. But in the end, I was able to put enough money in the bank to survive another six months. That money enabled me to save PKS, and that was all that mattered to me.

My leadership ability had been tested throughout the entire blue-roof contract. To jump on an airplane with a suitcase but no equipment, land in an unfamiliar environment, and take charge of hundreds of people I'd never met in my life was a daring bit of business. But helping all of the people who had survived a terrible tragedy was also rewarding. I felt like the mayor of Pensacola canvasing for votes. I shook hands with two thousand homeowners, assuring them that their roofs would not leak until the adjuster arrived, and I kept my promise. What was more, I did all of this with no infrastructure. I built an infrastructure by the end of the project, though. I hired three full-time personnel and a few part-timers. During my stay in Pensacola, I mapped the region, networked with anyone that would talk, and planted my first major footing into the federal market place. This capital project would lend importance to my near future. More importantly, this first real exposure to the Army Corps of Engineers was the credibility I desperately needed.

At the end of my roofing contract, I suffered from exhaustion, having worked 12 to 18 hour days for 87 days straight. My need for sleep was intense. The whole experience had been really challenging. Granted, I was young and had the fortitude to do anything. I was ready to do what I needed to make PKS work. My experience being a Marine definitely prepared me for the worst. But this business stuff was not going to be easy, especially if I had to fulfill every role in my young company. First, though, I slept for three days.

Afterwards, I worked on my business plans and goals. As I discussed earlier, I received my 8(a) certification from the SBA, but I was not really sure how to use it yet. The rumor was that an 8(a) company could walk into a federal agency and be awarded a "not to exceed 3.5 million dollar set aside contract" with the government. I read the rules and regulations every day, trying to figure out how I could get one of these mysterious contracts. Where would be the best fit for PKS? Where would I have the best opportunities? Pensacola seemed like a good start.

I decided to continue operating in Pensacola, leaving Ken to conduct roofing sales. After all, we had 2,000 names and phone numbers of homeowners who would all need new roofs. Why? We nailed plastic to every one of those homes, and you know by now that I keep my contact information. I started remodeling and roofing as many houses as I could. I assigned Ken to work in Pensacola while I pushed business back in Virginia. I partnered Ken with a local homebuilder who would allow PKS to work under his license for a fee. (I'll call him Willis). With all the insurance money and federal aid flowing in, Pensacola seemed like a mini-boomtown. While Ken kept business going in Pensacola, I decided to figure out how to get one of those multi-million dollar sole-source contracts. I had everything set up perfectly, or so I thought.

It wasn't long before trouble was on the horizon. The money I was investing in Ken and my part-time staff just was not paying dividends. PKS was spending $15,000 dollars a month on this startup operation with the promise of $25,000 a month in return. I watched invoices being sent to Willis, but PKS was not being paid for them. I inquired numerous times with Ken, but he only gave me the run-around. By March of 2005, I knew something was wrong.

I took a surprise trip to Florida and showed up at the office where Ken was supposed to be working. He wasn't there. I inquired for his whereabouts to no avail. Before I dialed Ken on the phone, I decided to see Willis. As I pulled up to his vacant building, I noticed the empty parking lot that a few months ago had hundreds of vehicles and people moving about. What had happened in four short months? As I read the bankruptcy sign on Willis's door, I was heartbroken again. I knew that I had just lost $40,000 in startup costs for Pensacola plus the $30,000 I'd spent in maintenance. I would never get paid now. Composing myself, I drove to Ken's hotel room, the one that I was paying for, to confront him. When I got to his room, he was dressed in his skivvy shirt and slacks.

"What's going on, Ken?" I asked.

"Hey, Sean, good to see you, man," he responded. "You caught me taking the day off."

I did not mention that I had been to Willis's building. I simply asked, "So where are our payments for PKS?"

He said, "I don't know. I've called Willis a bunch of times. I was told that it would be any day now."

"Well," I started, "let's take a drive over to Willis's place and see what we can find out."

"Sure, Sean," Ken agreed. "Let me get a shirt on, and we'll go."

The one thing I don't like about liars are guys that will continue with the lie even though they know they are caught. Ken was in this position.

He was nervous on the drive over. He kept telling me how swimmingly things were going. I already knew that the Pensacola PKS office was closed and I that would have to find another way to succeed. We got to Willis's office, where the sign was still hanging on the door. I knew that he was aware of what had happened and that he was lying. He feigned disbelief and sorrow at knowing we were not going to get paid, never admitting that he failed to warn me. He was a man with no integrity. Ken was going to ride the gravy train until I stopped it. Well, his ride was over.

Immediately, I let everyone on my payroll go. I attempted to pick up the pieces as I took four steps backwards in time. My resources were low, and now I was down to three months of working capital with only a few jobs to do to bring in more capital. I knew I was in trouble. The next few months would make me or break me all over again.

I had to put Pensacola behind me. It had been a great achievement, but it also was an epic failure where precious dollars were squandered on a man that talked the talk but failed to walk the walk. I told myself: *Never give up; just stay on mission.* I had to find that million-dollar contract. I just had to. Time passed quickly. I began to prepare for my first federal marketing meeting after a friend of mine introduced me to Jack, the USACE small business chief in Norfolk, Virginia. He was my first target.

One thing I'd learned about marketing was the importance of a marketing brochure and a website. Since the Internet age began, most potential clients would check out your website. The value of a website is truly unlimited as marketing goes; it's the modern day storefront. No one wants to shop at a poorly-built storefront. It should be enticing, but not so busy it makes a client sick. With a few clicks, it should supply critical information, the background of the company, and the contacts of key personnel. It should also have the most recent, relevant job descriptions as well.

So how was I going to build the PKS website ahead of my first federal meeting? To me, it was going to be easy. I would post my resume and provide short, graphic descriptions of my personal past performance and history. I opened a Word document, titled it "Anthrax Attacks U.S. Capitol," attached a photo, and said, "Personnel assigned to project provided X and accomplished Y." Then I gave the value and the project value, etc. I did that for all the recent jobs I'd worked.

My reasoning was simple: I had very little corporate experience but lots of personal experience. My resume became PKS's resume. While it appeared my company did the project, in reality *I* sold the job, managed it, and worked it. The experience was mine, and anyone who hired PKS would get the benefit of Sean Jensen's experience. This method of marketing was legal, and if anyone said I didn't do the work, I would point to the description that said "personnel from PKS performed the work described." Some clients later challenged me on this decision, but for now I had to build a brochure.

My marketing line at the time was, "We are not Halliburton. We are a small can-do company if you just give us a chance." I also introduced Polu Kai in a way no one had seen before. I made the ocean and Hawaii's beauty central to my company's core mission, which embraced the ethos of native Hawaiians, sharing my Ohana (family) and Aloha (love) with all. I determined to treat our clients, staff, and vendors like family, with love and respect.

My story was just beginning, but surviving two years in business had been no accident. I learned about myself while I was shaking all those hands in Pensacola. When the homeowners saw the leader of the group performing the work at their houses, many of them welled up with tears of joy and thanks. By the same token, when we screwed up, as we did from time to time, I personally assured homeowners that I would take care of the problem. The first step to being a leader and a CEO is taking responsibility. That ability to look someone in the eye and own your work and your company's work makes all the difference between leaders and followers. I was a leader, and I knew I could lead PKS to success.

I met Jack, the small business gatekeeper at the district headquarters of the SBA in Norfolk, VA. I was very nervous at first. I'd heard that if Jack gave you a thumbs up, you would be in a good position to get a contract. I wore Dockers and a short sleeved, collared shirt.

Let me just pause to say that I can't stand suits. I am at my most uncomfortable when I am in a suit. They are stuffy, in my opinion. I have them, but I don't like to wear them. My consistent goal in life is be comfortable. I am a boots & chutes kind of guy. And let me tell you, you are going to be much more effective pitching someone if you are comfortable. If you do construction, demolition, and dirt work, you may want to look like you actually do that kind of work. That's my opinion. You don't have to look like a bum; there are plenty of ways to dress well and comfortably. Most of the clients you meet in civil service (unless you're on Capitol Hill) will be dressed that way, especially in the GS-13 and under category.

Look at it this way. Do you want to hire the guy who's wearing a three-piece suit to mow your lawn, or do you want to hire the guy who looks like he knows how to turn on a lawnmower? I know that my reasoning may be hard for some people to hear, but it's my blunt opinion. It worked for me.

Here's another piece of advice. It's good to be early. I learned that habit in the military. Giving yourself extra time ensures that you will be mentally and physically prepared.

I arrived about an hour early to the meeting, giving me some time to collect my thoughts. Jack greeted me in the lobby, where he got me badged in to go upstairs. I had a five-page brochure that outlined my services and capabilities. Feeling good about PKS and having confidence in my skills, I began to preach. After I gave my sermon, Jack asked me a simple question. "How big is Polu Kai?" Arrrgh! That was the question I feared the most.

I answered, "You are looking at Polu Kai!"

He smiled and said, "Pretty impressive for one guy. That has to be the most honest answer any small business owner has given me in 30 years of doing this kind of work." As we talked, he found out that I was a veteran. He let me know that he was, too, and that he had served in Vietnam.

My love of history and study of military history gave me a huge advantage as we spoke. He asked if I had any disabilities from the service. I said that I had – I had gotten hurt several times during my service. After this meeting, I got benefits from the VA because of this talk. We discussed the importance of adding "service disabled" to the veteran status on my card. He told me about the rules and special legislation signed by President George W. Bush in 2003. The law allows a sole-source contract that does not exceed $5 million dollars to be written by the Veterans Affairs Department to an established service connected disabled veteran owned and controlled business. That official designation is service disabled veteran owned small business (SDVOSB).

As my mind ran down the road of possibilities, I knew that this was a special meeting and that Jack was going to be another mentor. We spoke for two hours. He educated me on the 8(a) program and the service disabled veteran program. In the end, he told me that I was a little bit too small of a company and that he would have trouble convincing anyone we were able to perform, due to our size. He did tell me that if I got a little bigger and had some more corporate past performance, he would give me a chance at one of the sole-source IDIQs (indefinite delivery, indefinite quantity contract).

Despite leaving the building without a contract, I was not disenchanted but inspired by knowing that I could get one down the road. Jack was a man of his word. I could tell. I would come back to him after I got the experience he requested.

Summertime of 2005 was coming on fast. I tried to put Pensacola out of my head and stay focused. I was on my own still and struggling with the loss of revenue in Florida. My business bank account was almost dry again, and I knew I was going to have to find a job soon. I needed to make a major move.

In August, something big was brewing off the east coast of Florida. Hurricane Katrina was moving towards the Gulf of Mexico with a vengeance. Earlier in the summer, I had borrowed $10,000 from my friend Harry to keep the company moving. I had a lot of irons in the fire but no takers. I was beginning to get disheartened. The 8(a) contracts were not panning out, and the little jobs were barely making ends meet. I wondered if I could repeat the initial success of 2004 and be called in to help with Katrina damage. If I was called, I vowed that this time would be different. I had learned after Hurricane Ivan what to do and what not to do. I changed direction and began to focus on preparing for Hurricane Katrina. Life at PKS was about to get interesting.

Hurricane Katrina struck with a vengeance on August 29, 2005. I started calling all of the prime contractors (primes) from the previous year to get involved. Their phones were dead. No one was picking up, probably because they had all learned how to be profitable from the previous four storms that hit Florida in 2004. What would I do now? How could I become part of the federal workforce that was going to respond to this massive catastrophe? The population would need help, just like I witnessed in Florida. I wanted to be a part of the help. My experience had to mean something.

I can tell you from experience that when you are the victim of a catastrophe, the resources to rebuild must come from outside your area. When there is no electricity, gas, or water service, the impacted population begins to change for the worse quickly. The National Guard arrives to help, and they are also critical to maintaining order. If you watched the TV and witnessed the dramatic events at the Superdome, you understand. Multiply the sorrow you felt by 1000 times. That feeling is the one you have when you get to the impact area and meet families who have lost everything. I saw the devastation firsthand during Ivan. Pensacola looked as if it had been carpet-bombed by B-52s. But a week passed before I received a telephone call from an old friend.

Here's another *Sean life lesson: I always say that if you respect your competitors in business, you will meet great business partners along the way.* Relationships matter, and a good partner can become a lifelong friend.

You know these friends because you can go two years without saying a word and then pick up the phone and start talking as if you'd spoken yesterday. I made many friends like this in my career. The one who called me the Sunday morning after Katrina hit, Eric, was a fellow jarhead working in a large response company that I'll call LRC. Eric had served as a gunnery sergeant in the Marines and was a well-known player in the emergency response field. He'd worked his way up the civilian ranks just like I did. His enthusiasm for his profession was unmatched in my eyes, and he was also loyal to the brink of insanity. At the time, Eric was the friend I really needed. He had no fear of success. When he wanted something from you in business, you would rarely say no; he was just that kind of guy. I credit Eric with giving me a once in a lifetime opportunity after Hurricane Katrina.

"Hey, Sean," he started. "You know that blue-roof stuff you did in Pensacola?"

"Yes, Eric. What's up?"

"I just told the Air Force that we could do the same thing for them at Keesler AFB."

"You did?" I replied. "What company are you going to use?"

He laughed. "Yours, of course!"

My adrenaline began flowing, and my heart rate sped up. I knew that this project would be the one to break PKS into the big leagues. I wrote the proposal out on white paper, using the previous year's rates. Knowing that I'd have no time to negotiate and that this work would be urgent and compelling, I bet my company's life the government would accept the previous year's rates, already negotiated with other contractors. That way they could justify the procurement. All government solicitation must have a cost and price justification. I knew that the Air Force would be no different.

Katrina hit Louisiana and Mississippi like a nuclear bomb, and Keesler Air Force Base sustained a major hit. Eric told me that I would have to put 2 million square feet of tarp down in seven days and that the entire base housing would have to be blue-roofed. At the time, he did not know that I had only $12,000 left in the bank. I wasn't even sure if my Ford Explorer would make it down and back. He told me, "You're a Marine. Figure it out. I will have a subcontract to you this afternoon." True to his word, the subcontract arrived within one hour.

Even though I was the sole employee of Polu Kai Services, I was going to take on Katrina. With no resources and no personnel, I called Ken in Pensacola. He had lied to me before, but I was desperate. I decided that I needed to give him a second chance in light of the situation. He would bring another person in as a consultant. I called Harry, the guy who had loaned me $10,000 to keep PKS afloat, and I asked him to quit his job and become a vice president with my firm. I told him that I would also pay him back his investment through this mission. Then I called my previous subcontractors from Hurricane Ivan, and I hired my sister-in-law, Barbara, to be an administrator for PKS. In 24 hours, I had 400 people moving towards Keesler Air Force Base. Even my wife jumped in to help. This job was the big one. Keesler was going to be an epic success. Being a US Marine, I did not consider failure an option.

My wife always insisted on one condition for my small business adventure: No borrowing equity from the house. She changed her rule that day. We bought a brand new F-250 Diesel for me to go to Keesler. And we borrowed $30,000 from the house to fund the initial purchase of the wood I needed. The truck would have the range and ruggedness I needed to survive this battlefield. Having learned from Ivan, I convinced the Air Force to let us sleep in the vacant barracks and to provide fuel for our trucks. I would not operate from a tent city this time. I'd already witnessed the medieval encampments from Hurricane Ivan. This time, PKS would be squared away. Or so I thought.

I learned that we had seven days to put up the tarp. Ken and the other consultant arrived on the first day, and the work crews started to straggle in. I encountered a problem immediately. Ken and the consultant were not moving fast enough. Clearly, they did not have a clue how to handle the situation. With no flights in and out of the immediate vicinity of the Gulf Coast, I knew I was in trouble. I would have to drive and get there fast. Eric's boss called me and told me that I'd better get my butt down to Keesler or I was going to regret it. He said that nothing was getting done. Harry and I drove all night from Fairfax, Virginia to Biloxi, Mississippi. Besides the mass destruction, I had to face mass confusion with my hastily-assembled team. When I arrived, I jumped out of the truck and went directly to Eric's boss, head of LRC. I knew I was in trouble. He gave me a map and told me what had to be done in the next 4½ days. I assured him that the job would be done.

I had four of my best sub-contractors working with me. Three of them were key contractors from Hurricane Ivan. I had trained them personally during that mission, and they knew what to do. I laid out the situation and told them that we would finish this work in 3 days, not 4. They jumped into action. I decided to deal with Ken later. He'd screwed me again.

As I moved around the base, I worked the front lines. I had not slept in 24 hours, and I would not sleep until the Keesler work was done. In a few hours, I had the first 20 of over 1,700 houses done. PKS was not supposed to work at night, but that didn't stop me. We worked until 1 AM. Who was going to mind? The houses weren't occupied.

We worked 18 hours a day, leaving just enough time to sleep, eat, and work. By the third day, we covered the entire base housing project, installing over 2.5 million square feet of blue poly tarp. LRC was amazed!

I went back to Pensacola to await the outcome. I had invoiced over $2,000,000 worth of work in 7 days. I had finally landed the big one. The president of LRC called me.

"Sean, when are you planning to pay your sub-contractors?" he asked.

I replied, "As soon as I receive payment from you, I will begin issuing checks."

He then asked, "How big is your firm?"

I told him the truth. "We are five strong."

You could have heard a pin drop.

"Son, you have cojones!" he finally said.

He immediately advanced me 30% of the $2,000,000 he owed me. True to my word, I began paying the subcontractors (subs). I took the most amazing risk, and when all was said and done I grossed over 40% profit, far more than I'd expected. PKS gained this profit because of our incredible efficiency.

PKS was on the map. We had pulled off what many thought was impossible. *If I can do a job like Keesler with two employees and a few part-timers, I can do anything,* I told myself.

Try to imagine covering a couple of thousand housing units in seven days. You might fall over thinking about it. But if you trust yourself, know what support you have, understand what you want to achieve, and can see over the horizon, anything is possible. I hired a roofing company to roof my house many years ago. 1900 square feet, and it took 6 guys 2 days to do. We did the equivalent of 300 houses a day to finish the job! I think that great achievement goes back to seizing opportunity when it presents itself.

The best part of the accomplishment was being able to see it from the air while flying over the base in a Marine Corps CH-53 Super Stallion Helicopter. The lieutenant colonel overseeing flight operations was kind enough to give me and my team a lift over Keesler AFB and to send me pictures of the work.

I had always imagined what success looked like. I lived vicariously through other leaders who took risks. I managed jobs for them just as terrifying as this one. Failure was always around the corner, but not this time. I took the battlefield. The question I had to ask myself now was: *Can I build a real company?*

It is true that without risk, there is no reward. And it is true that it takes money to make money. But I wasn't operating without a safety net. My wife had a full-time job. I had the knowledge and experience to get a job on the outside. I knew in my heart that I would have to stay disciplined and focused on the ultimate goal: sustainable work and sustainable revenue. The smart guy knows that when you have a big profit, the tax-man cometh. After I paid all my debt and all my vendors, I made sure to pay the tax-man. The quickest way to be shot out of the sky is to not pay the taxes.

Chapter 6:

Storm Salvage

Sean P. Jensen

CRAZY as it sounds, opportunity would knock twice. Now that I was already positioned in Pensacola a second storm, Hurricane Rita, was moving in the direction of Louisiana. This one packed a punch west of New Orleans, hitting Sulphur, Louisiana.

However, Hurricane Rita was not as kind to me as Katrina was, and neither were the clients. When Rita hit, my phone rang almost immediately. An old friend (let's call him Buford) was on the line with an opportunity. Part of me told me to run when Buford called. He was working for a decent company (that we'll call DC), and he had blue roof work. The prime contract holder was what worried me. DC had a subcontract with one of those multi-billion dollar-a-year prime federal contractors (that I'll call PFC).

"The job's a breeze," Buford told me. "Just put up what you did at Keesler, and we'll all do well."

I was confident, and I was skeptical. That little voice in my head was yelling at me. PFC had been known to wreck small companies. I saw them work firsthand on major spill contracts in the past. Like a bad horror movie, PFC had notoriously destroyed many a small firm.

Here's another *Sean life lesson. Just know that no matter how many engineering controls you put in place and no matter how strong a contract you think you have, you have to make sure you have a shark suit ready when you swim with sharks.*

Buford assured me that this job was different and that PFC would take good care of DC and PKS – scout's promise. Now Buford is a company man and a known quantity in the emergency response business. His word means a lot to me, and it meant a lot to me back then. I knew he would do his best to protect my young company because DC needed us to put the roofs up. DC hadn't done this kind of work before, and they needed our expertise.

Thinking about the future of my company, I swallowed hard and called a meeting with my team. I met with my best contractors and filled them in with every bit of information I could provide so that there would be no surprises. I told them that my contract to them would be the same one I got from PFC. I dropped the fair warning clause about PFC's track record. Then I asked by a show of hands who wanted to go, and the contractors all raised their hands. They seemed prepared to follow me to hell and back.

Utilizing the flow-down clauses of a contract is really the only way to protect yourself in government contracting. It's a pretty standard model still used day. Tying yourself to the prime's bond is the other way. You have to make sure that the prime acknowledges you as a contractor performing work on its project. Those kinds of protections were about all I could do in this case.

PKS mobilized to Sulphur shortly after the meeting. By this time, my team consisted of seasoned veterans who had worked three hurricanes between them: Hurricanes Ivan, Dennis, and Katrina. We knew what we were doing. Unfortunately, the sharks had gotten to Sulphur before our group and divided up a great swath of the work already.

The thing you have to understand about emergency response work is that it is first come, first served. When the whole town is on fire, clients will pay just about anything to put the fire out. The premium money goes to those who have the immediate capabilities to accomplish the mission. That's not a bad thing, just the facts. If you're a day late, you can still get work. If you're a week late, you're in a whole other ball game. We arrived a week late because of contract negotiations, and the rest of the players were already playing ball.

The late arrival in Sulphur hit my team and me hard. PFC would not let us start work until we attended their safety training. Then there was a shortage of houses to tarp, followed by disorganization beyond belief. PFC owned the project and the rights to divide the work as they saw fit. I immediately understood that the pricing agreement for our services cost more than some other subcontractors. So PFC handed the work to the guys that were 10 cents a foot cheaper, claiming they were being fair all along the way.

Now I had to feed, house, and supply 200 men and women in what was basically a combat zone without work. It was an emergency response nightmare. On top of that, the work PFC did send our way was spread out across 200 square miles. So PFC effectively took me and my team out of the equation. I have no idea why PFC would do that. They made a big mistake since we had already recognized the game and found a way to stop them before we all got hurt.

DC was lead on the project, so I followed their company's managers even though these managers were wasting money by hiring too many people who didn't know what to do and by tolerating slow, slipshod work. Watching the poor leadership was torture for me. Three weeks into the project, PKS and DC were both taking a bath, losing money every day. The project manager

(PM) from DC pulled me aside.

"What are you going to do to fix this problem, Sean? We're bleeding dry here."

Incredulous, I looked at him and told him straight. "You have to step aside and give me the reins. It's not too late to break even or make a little money, if you give me the reins."

The PM looked at me and said, "OK, I'll trust you. The first thing we will do is have an internal project meeting with all of our personnel."

For weeks, I had been incensed by the lack of progress and the do-nothing attitude the men and women workers displayed on the project. It didn't matter if PFC was screwing us if we were already screwing ourselves. A five-person crew getting only one house a day done was a disaster. The next morning, I determined to change things.

PKS had ten leaders all sitting on the fence. They were pretty much set aside by DC's ten people, who were there to watch us. I told DC to cut their work force and stop killing their profit. We had everyone we needed to make this project work. I told them that I would meet with all 200 workers. I've learned that sometimes you just have to throw down the gauntlet. I politely told DC's leadership what I would be doing and explained that they may not want to attend my meeting if they were sensitive to my liberal use of language.

I know they don't teach field work vernacular in the leadership handbook, but I was dealing with some serious roughnecks. They were taking advantage of every situation and milking the job for a free paycheck. I understood the games they were playing and what was at stake for us and them if we did not turn the corner. So I gave it to them. I had hired a translator to speak Spanish to the Spanish-speaking workforce, and I addressed the entire crowd in a busted-up warehouse.

Although I do not like to holler at people, this group had it coming. I reviewed all the things they had done wrong during the last weeks, arming myself with the facts. I explained how to fix the problem, and I clearly gave them my expectations. Then I told them where they would be if they didn't. I told them that if they thought they were bad and could take me out, they should come get some. I was no joke, and I would show no quarter. I wasn't the guy to mess with. I warned them all that I would put them on the street, all of them at the same time if necessary.

After the speech, the PM came over and told me that I was insane and that the workers wouldn't listen to me. I told him to wait and see where things would go from there. I felt that my message had been received by the people who needed to hear it. The numbers came in from the day after my speech, and we had our best production yet. We could turn the corner.

Not all the workers listened to me, and that night I fired 70 of them. As a man of my word, I was not going to tolerate any more bullshit.

The mass firing had two effects. The first was simple: the men and women knew I was serious. The second and most immediate effect was that fewer people meant cost savings and better production. Not having to feed and house 200 people allowed us to give more work to motivated crews who then saw more money for their efforts. A lot of people didn't necessarily mean success; if the Marines taught me anything, it was that less is more. I quietly told DC to keep the personnel numbers they reported daily high long enough for us to get more work from PFC. They were not playing fair, and we needed to even the playing field.

I also made sure that KFC was delivered the next day to the remaining workers. I wanted them to know that I appreciated their hard work and that I would reward their success. I showed them the other side of hard work, and it definitely changed their hearts and minds. The team trusted me now, and I would use that trust to turn the situation around.

All I could say was, "Thank the Lord that I joined the U.S. Marines!" The only way I was going to get through this operation was to be more calculating and determined than huge and heartless PFC. I would have to fight my way through this project using all legal means necessary. A Marine NCO knows how to play that game. We learn it from generations of leaders who pass down mountains of knowledge. They are called drill instructors.

If I were to give you an after action report, like we do in the USMC, it would say mission accomplished. We installed over 800,000 square feet of tarp, protecting well over 500 homes from the elements. We worked in the Hurricane Rita disaster area under extreme conditions with zero deaths and zero injuries. I built my first trailer park to house my team, complete with water, sewer, and electric service. Disaster areas like the aftermath of Rita sometimes spun absolutely out of control. Some of the disappointing items from my experience included firing or removing over 100 personnel from my project and dealing with grown men drinking too much after hours.

I also captured an escaped con who turned out to be a convicted rapist. Somehow he infiltrated our camp and blended in with the other workers. We apprehended him and returned him to the police. I won't get into the details, but it was crazy.

We had massive problems with DC's crazy leaders taking care of their own buddies. And I had to return some stolen goods taken by local subcontractors, a group that I was told to contract. These were guys recommended to us by DC's personnel. I should have seen that problem coming. I made quite a scene, going to a pawnshop to buy back the stolen goods. It was the right thing to do. The subcontractor's crew ended up in jail, and the entire group of thieves were fired.

Ultimately, I was a very tired man at the end of the project. My workers were exhausted. Though it took a while to get their respect and remove the sand baggers, we accomplished the mission and got down to a fine crew. I learned that sometimes you have to fall down before you figure out how to go forward. Knowing about the pitfalls of the fog of war definitely helped me maintain my bearing during very tough times. PKS closed out the project with DC, and after I calculated my costs and expenses, I was right at the break-even point. I also had a shiny new project to showcase for my young company. I thought that the worst was over and I had survived the onslaught. But I was soon proven wrong.

Unfortunately, Buford's company was not in the same boat. They took a beating on the project because they overstaffed the project with people who didn't know what to do. DC was a much bigger company, the $100-million-a-year variety. So when I went to Buford for final payment, he told me that the PM wanted a discounted invoice. I later learned the hard way that someone can give you his or her word, and someone else can break it.

I told Buford that I could not provide a discount and that DC should pay me what my team and I had earned and invoiced. I found out that DC was not going to pay me in full. Instead, they just sued me for breach of contract saying that they lost money on the job. They should have taken responsibility for their own losses, which included the owner of DC taking a private jet from Chicago to the jobsite with his executives. DC was going to just take from me to cover what they wasted. It was a travesty, considering that I did the right thing by paying my employees and my contractors exactly what I had promised.

I learned that having a contract doesn't mean squat when you work for crooks. All of my success seemed to be very short lived. DC owed my firm $220,000. I had received some money from them during the project, about 60% of the job prior to that. However, the discount they wanted was $100,000, about half of which I owed to one sub-contractor and the rest of which were my direct costs. This discount was going to hurt. Now I was a dead duck. DC was going to steal the profit I needed to keep PKS going.

In the Marines we learn that there are levels of escalation in a fight. Sometimes it starts verbally. Other fights start in writing, while still others start with a shot across the bow. But some are just plain old sneak attacks that escalate the force from nothing to whammo in no time flat. As my daughter likes to say, "That escalated quickly."

My own personal Pearl Harbor showed up as a breach of contract lawsuit brought to my house by a process server. I got a lump in my throat as I read the provisions against my firm. DC was suing me in Chicago, a very long way from Virginia and a very long way from Louisiana. Apparently, I failed to read the fine print of forum selection clauses, and I was now trapped fighting a federal case in the Cook County, IL circuit court. Who knew that DC could do that? Not me. And as far as the actual suit was concerned, someone once told me regarding legal matters that when the facts are not on your opponent's side, they can just make them up. That's what DC did.

Even though I knew trouble was coming, I had no idea that DC would sue to steal from my hard work. Since you don't get to punch people in the business world without getting in some kind of trouble, criminal or otherwise, you have to arm yourself with an advocate to throw the punches for you. I would be damned if I let those crooks steal from me and my family; so I hired an advocate, the best guy I knew. He was the same lawyer who had sued a previous client and got him to pony up over a similar issue. Who better to have on your side in a David-and-Goliath fight than the guy you just watched beat up another giant? I gave him a call, and he agreed to take the case.

You remember the talk about escalation of force? When someone comes at you hard, effectively pointing a gun at your head, you can do one of two things: fight or flight. Fight is not always what I prefer, but my uncompromising principles led to my decision. I knew I was in the right; so I chose to fight. I knew that one of the best ways to get your opponent's attention is to sue his business interest. In this case, that was PFC. I retaliated with over whelming force for my three-person company. I sued PFC, its bonding company, and DC in federal court. I sued the PM by name as well.

Here are a few things you need to know about suing a multi-billion-dollar business or even a large business doing a hundred million dollars a year in revenue. First, that company didn't get to that level because they were lucky. They have the resources and ability to crush or destroy most of their competition already. Second, they don't care about you unless you have something they want. To them, a guy like me is an annoying housefly who must be swatted. I still believe that sometimes today. Third, the best way to get rid of a small company suing you is to overwhelm their resources so that they can't fight with the truth. This happens through lots of legal motions that cost the little guy time, effort, and money. Sometimes, this approach will get the little guy to back down or quit the fight. Fourth, always remember that most of the time the big guys have the money to pay you; they just don't want to pay it. That was the case with my lawsuit.

Rumors soon spread about many small companies working the hurricanes getting screwed over by the large primes. Rita was no Keesler. The post-Katrina and post-Rita responses were shaping up to be political nightmares for the big boys. Most companies took the option of discounting their invoices, choosing to walk away hurt and hungry rather than to be crushed.

Not me - I was going to fight to hold these huge firms accountable. PFC and DC never thought that a three-person company would be able to take them on. I wasn't trying to prove a point, but I knew that if I walked away, I would set a terrible industry precedent for myself. Being a pushover would surely tarnish my reputation forever.

When I met the opposing counsel at a hearing in Chicago, I told the lawyer that PFC and DC were going to pay and that I would die before I let them get away with their treachery. I wasn't threatening. I was promising his defeat. "You shouldn't pick on a U.S. Marine. You just don't know what kind of response you are going to get. We are not quitters," I said, as my lawyer moved me away.

Business is not just business; it's always personal. That opinion may be hard to swallow, especially for professionals who read this book. But business is personal when you have everything on the line: your house, your life savings, and your honor and integrity. So for all sides of business, the good or bad, you take responsibility for the agreements you make.

Unfortunately for me, many of the four items I noted about suing a big company were coming true. My counsel was quickly depleting my funds, and the big boys seemed ready to keep me away from my day in court by dragging the process out as long as they could. If I could get to a federal judge, I knew that I would win, because I could prove that I did the work and that DC contractually owed me for those services.

I did everything I could to stay relevant. I wrote DC's board of directors; I showed them their own ethics policy. I planned to go public in the press, something I don't usually recommend, but I was desperate. The stakes were very high for my family and me. For almost 2 years I never strayed from the fight. Eventually, the big boys ran out of continuances and motions to dismiss, and a federal judge set a date for a jury trial. Just like that, the big boys decided that they wanted to settle.

If you are multi-billion dollar firm being sued by a small business for the paltry sum of money they owed me, you're going to look bad. The other side knows this. Once the journalists find out about a hurricane-related case, they'll write headlines saying that the small guy is getting screwed by the big guy. It's a public relations nightmare, especially when the big boys are trying to win a popularity contest every day. You don't get popular beating up the little kid at school.

The battle took two years of my life, but I ended up with a settlement out of court. DC paid me, and I paid my vendors in full and took care of my lawyer. Looking back, I would not change my actions. But before I made my decision to fight, I would have taken into account how slow justice moves in the real world. I thought that the courts would just say, "OK, you're right!" and DC would pay me. After all, the facts were on my side. That was not the case, though.

With the settlement, I considered myself vindicated and victorious. After all, if you believe you're right, you don't go as far as DC went legally to protect themselves and then up and pay. DC had all of the cards and all of the money. That didn't matter now. The time I spent on the case and the time and money spent by my attorneys cost me five times more than any discount DC wanted me to take or any money I may have gained by winning if I insisted on a trial. Besides, I could have lost everything and been liable under their lawsuit against me for attorney's fees and damages. Sure, I won the battle, but I almost lost the war.

Here's another *Sean life lesson: read your contracts carefully, even if they are a thousand pages. If you can't understand the contract, then hire an attorney or someone with commensurate experience to review it.*

Many companies and many agencies figure that you won't read your contracts. The few hundred bucks you don't spend up front could cost you hundreds of thousands in the end, maybe even millions, even if the facts are on your side. So weigh the invisible costs from your endeavor. Refrain from launching legal battles at all costs, because nobody really wins. I make every effort to settle before I draw swords.

Chapter 7:

Changing Tack

Sean P. Jensen

FROM December 2005 to December 2007 while my legal battle raged far from home, I lost most of the equity in my firm and drew near the doorstep of failure. The Keesler project seemed like a dream gone by. Winning a few projects along the way, I managed to build a little. But the time lost prevented me from sailing forward free and clear. Polu Kai was mired in a backwater, and I would have to change tack to fill our sails.

By this time, I had won my first few SBA contracts and was steadily planning my next three years. Those contracts were a great past experience that I lodged in my memory. Unfortunately, time was not on my side. It never is when you're running a business.

My observations of other leaders over the years had taught me many important lessons. *Sean life lesson: if you can't build something fast enough, buy it or lease it.* For me, trying to build a company from scratch, I took this lesson to mean that I needed to do what was possible rather than what was ideal.

I never imagined myself as a great leader with thousands of loyal followers. Nor did I imagine what my own company would someday look like. I mean, who would want to be part of it? What kinds of people would share my goal of commitment to success?

I had seen that building a business from scratch is not for the faint of heart. While I found great success in my three years in business, I still was finding my way. The clients who interviewed me usually didn't want environmental companies; they wanted construction companies. If they wanted environmental companies, they wanted ones with the very best of an expensive talent pool: engineers and scientists and the like. That kind of human resource would be kind of hard to fake for a guy who knew he only had three people and a picnic basket. The prevailing winds in my market had changed, and I needed to change tack to pick up a kind breeze.

Because emergency response companies come and go, I would have to diversify to be successful. My past experience, prior to starting my company, was feast or famine. Hurricanes didn't hit every day. Serious storms were a part-time gig. So how was I going to build a company that consumed few resources and only had a few contracts? I was not going to despair, and I was not going to wallow in the mud, waiting for work to land me. I determined to find like-minded businesses or successful individuals who wanted to make a living as badly as I did. In my case, I found a partner.

Before I get into business partners, let me digress a little bit. For a guy who just recently started a company, living the dream and then almost losing everything in a fight with Goliath, I considered 2002 through 2006 to be some of the most hair-raising years of my life. I worked seven days a week, and I was gone from my own family almost a year, building my business on the front lines while I lived in one crappy motel after another. I learned a lot, but I couldn't seem to get over the hump. Much more happened that I have not shared. If I told every story that happened, I would have to write volumes of books.

My thoughts, lessons, hopes, and ideas swirl around the major events that happened to me and my company. My hope is that, if you are a small business owner, you are comparing notes with me. If you're thinking about starting a small business, I hope you will heed my advice. You had better protect yourself. After all, I still run a company, and I continue to face new battles every day. If you are going to do anything in business, hopefully you will read and learn from my mistakes and successes, finding a way to impact your own life positively.

Partners to me are relationships built out of personal trust, shared goals, and honest principles. Whether you're married, supporting a spouse, raising a family, or assigned to a fire team inside a platoon of Marines, you need partners. Even adversaries and competitors can be partners. Without partners, trade would be virtually nonexistent. Partners don't have to know each other to make agreements. They just have to trust the other party to trade, buy, or sell labor, supplies, goods, or equipment to each other. One thing all partnerships require is commitment to the agreements they make. To be a truly successful relationship, both parties must trust and be willing to compromise. Building partnerships is paramount to success when you are a small business. It is the quickest way to set up a buffet for your clients. The more partners you have, the bigger the buffet and the more services you can provide. There is always added risk to taking on partners, and you must carefully weigh the reward in any venture. But my story would not have come to fruition had I not believed in partnerships.

The year 2007 was really a turning point for me personally. PKS had a lot of irons in the fire. Settling my lawsuit made life seem easier. I no longer had to worry about what might happen there; I was glad that it was done. During the time I fought it, I rededicated myself to my goal of building and expanding my business. I just did not have enough work, and finding more was becoming exceedingly more difficult without other service offerings. My early successes and early setbacks stayed on my mind as I tried to create more opportunity for my fledgling firm.

The business world can be quirky. When you're successful, everyone wants to talk to you. They want to be your pal. It is not unlike being picked to play kickball in elementary school. If you are a great kickball player, you have no problems landing a spot on the team. But friends are few when things don't go well. In your personal life as an adult, you can quickly determine who your real friends are if you tell them you're broke and need their help. Take a head count after that. It's funny but true.

I did have an early backer in PKS. My vice president, Harry, contributed his time, resources, and dollars. He had worked with an 8(a) company before, and after the hurricanes he was a small-percentage stock holder. I gave this share of Polu Kai to him based on his early contributions. He knew how to be successful, and he helped me out wherever he could. While I believed in him, my faith in him had become wary. He struggled with the big firefight against DC. It made everyone nervous. At one point, he asked if we both should get part-time jobs, because the pay with PKS was so low then. I told him that he could get one if he desired, but he shouldn't bother being a partner if he wasn't willing to make the sacrifice. He stayed steadfast, although he certainly lacked the vision I wanted him to have. His wavering faith never stopped me from seeking new work and moving forward.

I'd started seeking partners in early 2006, having thought about this expansion long before PKS fought the big boys. By 2007, I had a potential candidate on the line. Harry had met the VP of a firm based in Florida, coincidentally located where I grew up. The company was a former SBA 8(a) contractor. Oscar, the guy running it, was by all accounts very successful. A shrewd businessman, he understood the true potential of the SBA program, and he knew how to use it. But he wasn't fond of spending his money; if Oscar ever took a risk, he would risk as little as possible and ask for as much as he could get.

He had what I needed, employees and infrastructure. The employees he had were all trained in federal government contracts, and they understood what was required to get the job done. I had what Oscar didn't, though: access and a successful vehicle. The only thing getting in the way of our partnership was his opinion of my firm.

Oscar told me that PKS wasn't worth the paper it was written on. His lack of tact empowered me. I wasn't offended. I knew we were not a rich company. In fact, I appreciated his bluntness. He knew better, though. He knew that PKS could bring him value, and he was very interested.

I told Oscar that he would have to take a backseat, and I insisted on his full support in any merger. He really wanted to get as much as he could for as cheap as he could because he knew that with my background and credentials my company could be a gold mine. Oscar talked a lot about his net worth and how smart he was. I was the new entrepreneur with little experience compared to his. He didn't have to say it; I got the picture. He had connections to the construction industry, primarily bonding companies to insure us and subcontractors that could do the work.

In my research, however, I found mixed messages about Oscar and his company. His last partnership had ended badly, and he had lost trust in people. We all had the "got burned" story, it seemed. Being cheated was like a rite of passage in business.

After what seemed like months of discussions, Oscar walked away from merging with my firm. He wanted too much from me, and our partnership would have jeopardized my status as an 8(a) company. While Oscar wanted to compromise a little, he wanted control. I just wouldn't allow that arrangement, and the SBA absolutely didn't allow it.

Here's another *Sean life lesson: When you are dealing with a tough negotiation, and you are trying to defend yourself from a shark, you have to use every asset available.*

In this case, federal law mandated what was allowed in an 8(a) business and a SDVOSB partnership. For starters, control of the day-to-day operations, as well as the strategic direction of the company, had to rest with the majority business partner. SBA rules were quite clear on that topic. Additionally, partners of previous 8(a) firms were limited in the amount of stock they could own: 20% ownership in the first five years of the program and no more than 30% after that. Oscar feigned ignorance of those rules, but I knew better. He hadn't survived nine years in the 8(a) program by being an idiot.

I needed to ensure that I did not hand the wheel of my ship to this guy, even though I needed the diversity and past experience of his company to help me with my master plan. So I used the SBA regulations to protect me with great success. Even after this rejection of my firm, I still thought Oscar was my best option for a partnership. His words about my company didn't mean anything to me because I didn't give them credibility. True, Polu Kai lacked resources and money, but that lack didn't mean we were not valuable. If we were so worthless, Oscar would not have kept talking to me after his rejection. But before too long, the tides of fortune would change with or without him. I was hell-bent on succeeding, and Oscar knew it.

A bit later, I learned about a big project in Florida right down the street from Oscar's office. As it turned out, Oscar had performed work there in the past. The VA hospital was an old important client of his. With the priority changing to hire Service Disabled Veteran-owned firms, the chief of contracting at the hospital thought PKS would be a great addition to his vendor team.

I convinced Oscar to put a joint-venture (JV) together with my firm to test my theory of success. To make a believer out of him, I had to show him that I would be successful with him. After a win with the VA, I was sure that I would see Oscar coming back to my door with a slightly different attitude. I also believed that he would compromise on the new relationship according to the rules, because he did understand them. A few weeks later, I received the news that the PKS JV had been selected for the project. I would say it took Oscar 20 minutes to call me.

This time, he called me with a little more humility and some excitement in his voice. He said, "We have to make this work. It's the real deal!"

Oscar would have a vehicle and a home for his employees by merging his company into mine. I knew the truth. He had been laying people off in his own firm because of bad economic times and lack of work. But Oscar was a smart guy, and I knew we could work together. Not long after the merger and arrival of the new employees, however, the construction real-estate market crashed, and the country fell into the Great Recession.

Despite the bad news, I knew that the potential for PKS was there and that the time was right for me to take PKS orbital. Armed with seasoned federal contracting employees and a new partner who had bonding connections and credibility from his past business relationships, I was ready.

I met my new employees in Tampa. I sat down and spoke to each for fifteen minutes. I could tell that I was going to have issues with some of them right off the bat. I am a pretty straightforward guy, and I am not scared to ask direct questions. For these guys and gals, I had three. How do you feel about joining PKS? Where do you want to go? Where do you want to be? Most answered cautiously, giving the party line answers: I am happy doing administration; I am happy estimating. That was fine. Some took the questions in stride and admitted to not wanting to do specific things. Of course, I knew they would move on sooner or later. Others let me know how important they were. They told me how I was supposed to handle them.

I'd walked into a zoo, so to speak. I spent the first six months of this merge taking out the bad apples and righting the wrongs. I learned that Oscar would not be the heavy. He would leave all of the tough calls to me. Whether that was on purpose or not, I will never know.

One person I brought over in the merger was the perfect match for me. Dawn was a division controller who had worked for my partner before me and as an executive in a Fortune 500 company before that. Sharp, talented, and extensively experienced in accounting and process management, Dawn would be the go-to person to build the internal highways where I was going.

Everyone set to task, knowing we were out to change the small business world. A few people in Oscar's company were keepers. Others needed holy water and a priest to exorcise them from my newly-merged business.

I don't know why, but some people just have a chip on their shoulder. God forbid if you are successful and happy. If they aren't happy, they will play for sympathy and then act out, sending a bad letter or a bad email or saying something that will piss everyone off.

Unfortunately, one of the new employees, Alice, had the office on pins and needles all of the time, threatening personnel and then pretending like the consequences were someone else's problem. She happened to be the best friend of, let's just say, the right person's spouse inside the organization. She thought of herself as an untouchable. And I knew I'd have to deal with her sooner or later.

Chapter 8:

Smooth Sailing

Sean P. Jensen

BY the end of 2007, PKS had conducted more marketing, and we began enjoying a stretch of smooth sailing with wind in our sails. Polu Kai finished better than I thought it would. Before the merger was completed in September 2008, we faltered a few times with the new gang. By now PKS had offices in Falls Church, Virginia and in Tampa and Miami, Florida. We also had satellite employees working in New York and Kentucky. Finally, we were moving in a whole different way. I just needed to hire one more addition: someone who could sell like I could.

One thing you have to understand about the 8(a) program is that it is like a cult of personalities. It has its own language, its own lingo, and an underground of professionals and career politicians that stay in it forever. Because it's been around for a long time, it can point to many success stories, but there are many more failures. I like to say that the small business battlefield is littered with the bodies of dead 8(a) firms. Like any federal business program, it has many rules to keep people honest. It also has many pitfalls. If they don't play fairly, federal prison is where the really bad offenders go. Don't think about defrauding the U.S. government, especially in the SBA business development program. At the end of the day, I can think of no federal program in the world beside government grants that has such potential for success, as well as disaster.

As I explained, you pitch a government official on your capabilities, and if the stars align and you have the skills and abilities, you can receive up to a $4,000,000 contract. This kind of contract was the golden ticket, as many had explained to me. I didn't think too much about golden tickets. I was thinking about new and repeat business, sustainable business. I had won a few 8(a) contracts since 2005, but I had not won any races in the metro area of DC. I was a minority business owner for sure. The SBA had certified me. Yet I couldn't work in my backyard. The problem was, as I learned from one intrepid contracting officer, I wasn't black or Indian.

"How can you say such a thing?" I asked. "Isn't it illegal to discriminate?"

The contracting officer recoiled in horror. "Discriminate? We would never do that!"

"What the hell is native Hawaiian, then, chopped liver?"

I would have to find an end around. Apparently, I looked too white to be a minority. The damn thing is, when clients actually looked at our qualifications, they changed their minds. They asked us to put a presentation on for

109

a job on the basis of being a minority business. I would present clients with my capabilities and let them decide. That is how I would run my business from now on.

Thanks to President Bush signing the "Veterans First" bill, service-disabled veteran was added to the federal socioeconomic goals. Better than that, Veterans Affairs would be able to sole-source contracts to SDVOSBs. The US government has goals to set aside at least 23% of the federal dollars they spend for small businesses. I would fit into three categories: native Hawaiian, veteran, and service-disabled veteran for my service in the Marine Corps. My dear friend Jack was right when he told me to add SDVOSB to my card. Picking my company to do work was a good thing for government officials, because they got to check three boxes. They would get their small business credit. I had a better chance than the guy who wasn't a veteran.

Because of the new bill, there was a lot of outside pressure on PKS. A lot of companies and past 8(a) owners pushed hard on my young company, trying to tell me how smart they were and how they would all make me a millionaire if I lent my name, sat back, and watched them work. I didn't listen. I had my team, and I was in it to win it.

Swimming with business sharks can make any man nervous. You have to watch your Ps and Qs. Everyone is always looking for an advantage. If you have comments about a powerful contractor, it is best keep them to yourself. Lord knows, if you say anything bad about a government agency, you will get blackballed if the wrong person hears your words. I have seen it happen.

I prickled at the numerous offers. If this 8(a) stuff was so easy, why didn't people want to stick with their own companies? I got the impression that they weren't all living the American dream if they were trying to persuade me to bring them in. I would tell them all: "I have nothing you want. We are small, just a few people."

I needed a sales buffer, someone that could pick up the slack and be a first strike person. You see, I had two or three guys that could sell, but they were in Florida. I needed someone in DC. If this merger was going to work, I would need a big hitter.

I found that person in the nick of time. This professional 8(a) marketing group was courting me, constantly hitting me up for work. After a couple of meetings, I was sure they were a scam, but they kept coming. Finally, on their last push, I met a tall, very well put together black woman. She was a lady most days; but she had another side, a winning side. She knew her stuff! I was sure she was working for the wrong group. She needed to work with me.

Gail was an extremely sharp, likable woman who impressed the hell out of me (she still does, even to this day). She was connected with the government buyers in Washington. She could open doors for me, and she also had the ability to adapt and learn - a talent you rarely see in sales. Many people claimed they were top-notch salespeople and that they could help me grow PKS. From the beginning, they all turned out to be shams.

The only problem with Gail, however, was that I couldn't stand her bosses in the marketing group. They were very shady, and I refused to work with them. Every time I met them, they gave me the heebie-jeebies.

To get to Gail I had to go through them, and they were desperate to lock me down. Like always, some dude was trying to tell me that I needed him to control me. They pushed one contract forward, and we won it. Their contribution was nothing. I couldn't see their purpose.

Gail was doing the marketing, and as I would later hear from her, she wasn't being paid. They were changing the rules. That was it for me. I told them that I was done and that I didn't want any part of their business. Of course, they wanted a commission for the job that Gail had sold, and I had to pay it. Then I told them to lose my phone number. Gail and I had sales to do.

In our line of work as 8(a) service-disabled veteran contractors, we really had to put ourselves out there to get recognized. I had been to at least 12 conferences in 2007 and 2008 combined. Every bit of profit I made went into building and marketing Polu Kai.

Now the table was set. I had the marketing machine in place, and I had the staff to perform the work, courtesy of the merger's addition of personnel to my firm. And I had the past performance. The plan was simple: Gail and I would market the combined qualifications of native Hawaiian and service-disabled veteran to any government agency that would listen. We would do this like a wolf pack hunts prey. We would overwhelm them with quality people and quality work. When the USACE had their winter 2008 annual small business conference in Memphis, Tennessee, we would be there.

I was ready to sink some ships, and not just any ships. We were going after the battleships and carriers, which meant that any government small business chiefs and/or their deputies would be our primary targets. We needed them to tell us who the buyers were at the program level. We had a list, and we had prior relationships with some of the chief small business deputies already. The question was: Would they accept Sean and the new Polu Kai team?

Eight of us showed up to the conference. We had a booth and a plan. We would have to cover more than 1,200 attendees. We figured that there were a couple hundred government officials; the rest were company reps like us, trying to market their companies and crack the code as well. Our secret was manpower and Kona coffee. We didn't expect PKS to get a contract at the conference. We only expected to get past the gatekeepers like Jack and find the buyers. We did just that!

I had created a brand, being native Hawaiian. With family-type introductions and down-to-earth people representing the Polu Kai brand, we were different in the market place. By my observation, I did not have one native Hawaiian competitor firm at the conference. It was on.

The Kona coffee giveaway was a huge sell. Government workers and coffee seemed to go hand and hand. We brought some real characters to the table in Memphis. All of our people there were marketing or technical, and they knew how to party. Pretty soon the government types noticed how much fun we were having and started asking questions.

The story of the Hawaiian jarhead soon got around the government circles, and we were invited to make multiple presentations across the southeast and mid-Atlantic. On top of that, some of the large businesses noticed us, too, and we began to get offers to meet their government procurement representatives to see if we would consider partnering or subcontracting some of the work to them. We listened to everyone.

For the first time, I felt like PKS was going to chart a course around the world. All the principals of PKS were there, including Gail, whom I'd managed to bring on as a full time employee for PKS. Gail stood on her own, driving her friendships and business relations to PKS. She did exactly what I knew she would do. Harry, my first partner, was also there in full swing.

The crossovers from the merger included Randy, my newly-appointed vice president for the southeast region (a.k.a. my Cuban ambassador, because he was born in Havana, Cuba). Randy worked out of Miami. He was an excellent salesman and the cousin of Oscar, my new business partner. At 6' 3", Randy was the tallest Cuban I'd ever met. I joked with him that he must have been part of some top-secret communist growth experiment. Considered an 8(a) insider, Randy really knew the government and was strong in environmental cleanup and government contracts.

We had Jeanne, from the Tampa office, who was a very effective communicator. With her excellent presentation skills, she had been working her way up the ranks from receptionist to head of corporate bids and proposals. She was really a bright star at the conference, running the booth and providing the potential clients that raided our booth with coffee.

We also had Richard, who was not so impressive. Actually he annoyed me. At one point in our relationship, he thought I was going to throw him off a bridge. He just knew everything, and nobody likes a know it all. Oscar swore by him, though I didn't see why.

Last but not least, we had me. I shook every hand in the conference, just like I did with every homeowner whose house I blue-roofed in Pensacola after Hurricane Ivan. I put myself out there for all to inspect and question. I had my own relationships, and we used the team to show strength and experience at the conference. The Polu Kai story was turning into a good one. My direction to my team was simple. Make friends, and renew existing relationships. But do not compromise my integrity or yours. If you want to succeed, you need to perform!

That was what we were doing and what we intended to keep doing when we got the contracts. With the setback in 2006 and 2007 after Hurricane Rita, Polu Kai lost money and equity. The gross revenue was down to $1.7 million from the high of $2.1 in 2006. But I had faith in myself. I was facing a new challenge.

If you were on the outside looking in at PKS financials in 2008, you would have thought we were doomed. In 2008 we were still going backward, posting $1.2 million gross revenue at year end. I was unfazed. I knew in my heart I had something special in PKS. The merger would change the momentum. We nailed down a few VA contracts and picked up some 8(a) work to provide sustainable income through 2009. Starting to dig out of the hole felt great, and I was encouraged to have some quality talent around me.

That year we had our first true senior leadership meeting, and we set goals for 2009. We also found time to have the first bridging of our mid-Atlantic personnel and southeast personnel by holding a Christmas party in Florida. I traveled with the mid-Atlantic staff as a show of good faith. I wanted to show my commitment to my southern team. Everyone in the company attended.

My projection for 2009 was 5 million, with an upward projection in 2010 to 15 million. I believed we could bring in new work and add to the back log we had in 2008. You see, before anyone's arrival, I had already managed to secure several million dollars in new, multi-year contracts with the EPA in New York and Georgia. Polu Kai landed a bunch of small contracts in Langley AFB in Virginia, building a strong go-to relationship with the Air Force. We had more work coming in behind that with the Air National Guard. While all the new work had not been contracted to us yet, I knew it was coming. Coupled with Gail and my new group of seasoned vets, Polu Kai was going to become a formidable ship in the water. No one on my crew seemed to know how formidable we were going to be except me. My partners didn't buy into my projections. But all their caution did was motivate me to prove them wrong. Before I could do that, though, I would have to straighten up my crew.

Chapter 9:

The Polu Kai Crew

Sean P. Jensen

FOR a ship to sail smoothly, the whole crew needs to know their individual jobs, how those jobs relate to the ship's motion, and the ship's destination. They also have to be loyal to the captain. For me, my ship's crew were my employees. But they weren't just employees to me. I had purposed from the very beginning of Polu Kai to run the company in a Hawaiian way. I wanted my employees, as well as my clients, to feel like family – ohana. I wanted to treat them with love and respect – aloha. But some of my employees – my crew - couldn't embrace the company culture.

Newton's third law says that for every action, there is an opposite and equal reaction. To sustain the kind of growth I was projecting, PKS would have to build a chain of command along with the infrastructure to support my growing population of employees. The challenges of leading and supporting myself and 5 other people had now exploded with the 30 plus employees and consultants spread around the eastern half of the country.

I decided to task Dawn, my organization's secret weapon, with tearing apart our old accounting and project management systems. I wanted her to find a new system that would provide us with an administrative engine to grow. At the same time, 2009 would be the year I fixed some of the personnel issues in the firm. You see, the merger created a political dynamic with some southern personnel seemingly more loyal to Oscar and his team than to corporate in Virginia. This dynamic had to change. The folks in the northern tier were not much better at working with the south, either. The little alliances and cliques in the organization had to go; so I needed to put the bad actors off my ship.

I am not one to demand respect in my position. The Marines teach differently: a leader needs to earn respect. As they proudly advertise about the Marine Officers Candidate Selection program: "The Marines select you as an Officer; you don't select the Marines." The officers are little different from the enlisted corps in the recruiting and hiring process, and you must keep a sharp eye to see the differences. We are all Marines after all. As the president and managing member, I was the corporate officer, and how I would wield the power and authority I had was up to me. I preferred the non-aggressive route. After all, these employees were civilians, not Marines. Unfortunately, most of the employees were down in Florida. Some would need correcting, and others would need to move on.

One lady in particular was tormenting my Tampa office personnel: Alice.

Alice had never been happy with me in charge, and she let everyone know it. I could tell when we first met that she was trouble. Oscar knew she was trouble, too, but instead of dealing with her, he left the job to me. Alice's attitude and behavior to others was condescending, disruptive, and just outright mean. She preyed on the young admins and fought directives that I put out to move the company in the direction I wanted it to go. She was an antagonist.

They say you have to move quickly to cure a cancer. In the corporate sector, people like that can kill teamwork and quickly spread hate and discontent throughout a company, just like a cancer attacks good cells. Too often, good people will exit after they see an employee getting away with what Alice was doing.

At first, I verbally counseled Alice over the phone from Virginia. She had a favorite target in the office, a young admin. Alice bossed her around, saying things that would set this young admin off every day. She would make comments like: "Sean is going to be the end of us," and "I am not going to listen to this guy! Who does he thinks he is?" She'd spout all kinds of crap. That behavior from a grown woman who should have been more mature had become a habit. She had been with Oscar's firm for several years prior to the merger, but Oscar's leadership had never addressed her behavior.

Alice drew my ire again by berating a vendor who made a simple error. When the vendor took the time to write me a lengthy dissertation on how unprofessional she had been, I knew I had to put a stop to her negativity. I told Alice that was her last straw. She immediately had to change her attitude or find somewhere else to be. I put her on probation. Scuttlebutt (that's gossip for you non-seafaring folks) said she was complaining about me and anyone else in the company that was working to make PKS successful. I wondered at Alice's gall. *If you don't respect me, at least respect the position; after all, I am signing your paycheck*, I thought to myself.

Sure enough, lightning struck again, and Alice blew up at another vendor. This time she caused a problem with the drug testing company. I made my decision. I flew to Tampa to dispatch Alice from my company.

Dawn called me when I hit the ground. WWIII had broken out in the Tampa office. Apparently word had spread that I was flying down to fire Alice. Somebody called Alice to warn her I was coming, and the news sent her into a tail-spin rage.

Why the hell would anyone do that? I thought. *It's not like anybody can stop me from firing Alice.* By then, Alice was cussing me and anyone around her while she awaited my arrival. Meanwhile, my new Florida team was in for a demonstration from me on human relations.

Alice's conduct had been outrageous for a long time. The merger just made it worse. This lady had created a negative environment in the office that Oscar just ignored as if he were sanctioning the way his employees were suffering from this lady. He wouldn't fire her. Instead he hopped a plane to come to Virginia for a convenient meeting where he didn't have to deal with something he had let get out of control.

I met Alice in the Tampa conference room with Dawn and my newly hired HR consultant. I made sure I had multiple witnesses because I knew this confrontation was going to get ugly. I calmly pulled out the paperwork documenting Alice's behavior and giving her my reasoning for her termination. She started screaming and telling me how horrible I was. I thought to myself, *I could use a priest and some holy water right now.* It was crazy. Her ranting went on for about 15 minutes. Finally, I just told her that my decision was final and that she needed to pack her things.

I do not take pleasure in letting people go. The responsibility comes with the job. Some people make it easier than others.

The message I sent to my Tampa office was two-fold. The first part of the message was that I was in charge, and I would not hesitate to discipline. The second message was that I would not tolerate bullying in the work place. It was that simple. There was a new CEO in town who cared about each one of them. I think the employees realized that I cared about them enough to take care of this problem personally and to stop the madness plaguing their office. I would be lying if the air in the building didn't get a little lighter and the staff in the office didn't quietly cheer. With the southern operation, a few more employees would head out the door, mostly of their own volition. This was more than I imagined. If there was a third message I sent to the company, it was that I am an equal opportunity employer. I had my own Alice. Her name was Sally, and some thought that she was untouchable, as she had been friends with my wife for more than 20 years. But I do not play favorites, even for the ones closest to me.

While Oscar had the respect of his employees, he lacked the ability to deal with the challenges close to him. He was a smart man, a multi-million-

119

aire. But he was also using me to fire or remove all the people he didn't want to remove personally. I made him look better, because he was not the bad guy. I would also say he had no problem throwing me under the bus in this situation.

He knew Alice had to go. The advance warning to Alice was just another demonstration of what I would have to deal with down the road.

In my opinion, Oscar had a fear of personal conflict. He ran from it. However, I could tell that he had conflict resolution skills. Starting a business from scratch like he did, surely he dealt with bad employees. But now he seemed to be saying, "I am not the president. You deal with it!" I saw the writing on the wall. To protect myself and the firm, I would have to take on the tough fights in the future when it came to personnel.

Because my partner was not going to be much help, in the long term I would need to develop better middle managers to lead the team down south. If we were going to have folks running rough-shod around the southeast and Oscar was going to let them run, I needed to find some other leaders.

The merger forced me to cut people that were close to me. I cared about my employee Sally a great deal. Sally had been a good friend of my wife Nicole's. Sally dedicated herself to my early success, but she was not adapting well to the administrative changes Dawn was bringing to accounting and project tracking.

Sally's journey to my firm began with the mortgage industry collapse. I recruited people to be my admins who were out of work at the mortgage banking company where Nicole worked. I figured that their attention to detail, developed by working in the banking industry, would go perfectly with federal contracting.

Unfortunately, the thousands of pages of data that needed to be organized, reported, and submitted on some of the contracts I signed could demoralize most people. Sally embraced the challenge and worked hard to understand the work and keep up. But she was not qualified as a controller.

Dawn came from a Fortune 500 construction company as a division controller. She was a pro with an MBA and CPA under her belt. Sally was intimidated. While these mortgage banking folks proved to be useful in the admin process due to their extensive process management background completing bank loans, construction was a different world. I needed a strong, experienced leader to run the administrative and financial side of my business.

Sally couldn't let go. She was withholding company information from Dawn that disrupted my transition process. Ultimately, I tried to work her into a new position under Dawn. It didn't work out. Sally was living in the past where she could be relied upon to do everything I needed done on 10 contracts. Before, PKS was so small that was easy. But I was seeing the future, and it would be impossible for one person to do the work all alone.

I was sad when Sally resigned. After I accepted her resignation, she said later to Nicole that she thought I was bluffing and didn't think I would accept it. Nicole replied, "You should know better than to try and bluff Sean."

I trusted Dawn, and I let her set up the entire finance and accounting division of Polu Kai, providing her with the support she needed. I would let her find other qualified people and build her own team. From my perspective, I had no business in number crunching, and I needed to trust someone.

Polu Kai graduated from mom-and-pop status when we completed the merger and busted the 30-employee mark. I felt badly for Sally and for Alice. They weren't the only ones who would have to exit for me to create the success I wanted. Both of them were probably the most memorable people to me during that period of time. They tested my resolve as a leader.

They had a lot in common. Both were divorced from bad marriages. Both had family and personal issues. And both were single and trying to make it in the world. One was loyal to me and my business; the other was loyal to Oscar and his business. I knew there were deeper life issues with both of them, and there was not much I could do about that. I didn't quite understand why they fought me so hard against the merger and why they couldn't work into the new organization.

Something became clear to me during this time. The risk in this new relationship was not just Oscar; it was a certain group of people in the southern office who were loyal only to him. I got the feeling they thought I was a second-class citizen. They didn't like their boss being vice president to a guy in his thirties. Their disapproval didn't bother me while they kept a low profile. Besides, I knew where I stood on the planet.

My other employees knew, too. I could tell that the team was warming to me and they were embracing the new leadership style. I led from the front. I was a can-do guy, something they had not seen before. I was a Marine they were going to get to know personally.

We had enough office drama in those early months of '09 to kill a horse.

But cleaning up the office staff was necessary to achieve our future goals and make the workplace better. I continued to bring the mid-Atlantic and southeast operations together through personnel trips, eventually investing in a point-to-point video system so that they could speak face to face. PKS needed to operate as one unit and to pull from all of our talent simultaneously.

Just like in the Marine Corps, we needed an integrated fighting unit: troops on the ground to get the work done, command and control, coordinated logistics, and an organization and communications network to ensure mission success. We needed a real-time method of getting information in and out. That video system along with the new accounting and project management software would lead to millions and millions of dollars, I was sure. We just had to make the investments.

There are hidden pitfalls to any merger and acquisition. I suspect if I had more experience I would have realized that sooner. I tried to make everyone as comfortable as possible during the transition. I had taken on a great deal of risk bringing in a new partner and new employees. Ultimately, I had to eliminate some of that risk.

On paper, I was in complete control of the company. On the other hand, the politics made a much different story. Included in all of the crew changes, my first partner, Harry, wanted out. The risk of growth was too much for him; he was on the road and hitting the bottle pretty hard. His wife and he were going through a bad time, made worse by the early setbacks in the company. Now everything was coming to a head. Harry's wife would not risk her signature on the bond indemnity.

The bonding company requires the corporate principals and their respective spouses accept personal responsibility in the event of default or termination of a bonded construction contract. Essentially, you can't hide your personal financial responsibility. You've got to love insurance. The risk and cost creates a big incentive to complete each project.

Harry said his good-byes and tenured his resignation. His timing could not have been better. Since we were profitable, his payout was generous, more generous then what he initially invested, and well-deserved. A deal was a deal, and I would be true to my agreement. Harry wasn't adapting well to the merger anyhow. And if his wife wouldn't indemnify him, there was more going on than I knew about. I wondered if Harry regretted introducing

Oscar to me. Just when things were going well, he was going to leave. Maybe he was looking for an out for a while. Who knows?

One smart thing I did when I set up the company operating agreement was to include a buyout timeline. I knew that if I was successful and I had partners, a partner who wanted to leave could break the bank account by demanding his cash at exit. Heading off that possibility, I had the buyout terms set to monthly payments over 5 years. Harry took his buyout terms and left the company. When I made his last payment, I sent him a note. But even today, he has not spoken to me since the day he quit. He was very bitter- another casualty of change.

This time of growth and reorganization was crazy. I knew I would have to win the hearts and minds of many to be successful. I just thought they'd all belong to clients. I didn't realize that the hearts and minds I'd need to win included my own employees. Their hearts and minds became the most important for me to win.

The 8(a) minority contracting world, which was very small already, could get even smaller if you pissed off clients. I was going on my 6th year in business. My firm had not really been around long enough to piss off anyone yet. In fact, most of the clients we had were now beginning to come back and hire us for follow-up work.

Oscar was not as fortunate. He had made some powerful enemies out of a few past clients. They made it clear to me that they would not do business with my firm while Oscar was a part of it. This news came at the same time as his previous company, the one he built with an ex-partner, was out there trash talking him. While I knew there was some bad blood, having heard some of the rumors on both sides, I would have to steer the ship clear of the folks who didn't like Oscar. It was another unfortunate complication to our merger. Enemies I never thought I had became mine with the merge. Still, I believed I could survive the baggage Oscar brought to the table.

Sean P. Jensen

Chapter 10:

Familiar Shores

LOOKING back, I believe Polu Kai's biggest break in business came from the most unlikely place. In the summer of '08, just as the merger was coming together and the new systems and processes were coming on-line, Pensacola became the focal point for PKS again. During the 2004-2005 hurricane season, Pensacola was the place to be. It had been my forward operating base. During the time I had spent down there, I had been intrigued as to why more 8(a) companies were not marketing the area.

I had to know why. Marketing to a region eleven hours' drive from my house was a far reaching effort on my part. Once the hurricanes passed and the blue-roof and debris-removal work finished, it became a regular town again. It was weird how everyone seemed to move in for a short time and then move out, never to be seen again. The city had the beach tourism on one side, with NAS Pensacola picking up the rest of the attention. On the other side were rural agriculture and plant workers. I knew that the area did not have any obvious attraction to a federal contractor looking to make millions. The resumes and the workforce didn't lend itself to that kind of prospect. Without substantial commitment from clients or the good-ole-boy system to sustain your business, you were going to be a dead duck.

I learned that lesson in 2004 when I tried to set up contracts to repair homes damaged by Hurricane Ivan. I was run over and lost much of the revenue I earned working Hurricane Ivan by investing in bad actors like Willis and Ken. The people I trusted could not live up to their promises because the opportunity was not there. Even if you knocked on the right doors or knew the right buyers, guys like me would be run out of town.

But I was committed to Pensacola, and I was committed to having an operation there for a multitude of reasons. Even after the merger, everyone told me I was nuts. "You're not from around there. They don't give work to outsiders." I heard that kind of thing a lot.

People just didn't know that I was watering the seeds I had planted in '04, '05 and '06. I didn't try and explain it to them. I personally worked and lived along the Gulf Coast for months at a time during those years. Everywhere I went along the Gulf Coast I sought an opportunity to get on first base. From Florida to Texas, I personally managed my projects and met potential government clients on the ground. But I always seemed to play second fiddle to a large business. Whether I worked for them or they worked for me, it was hard work.

After Katrina, I landed a prime contract to remove trees from a bayou in Slidell, Louisiana. I was beholden to my sub because he had the heavy equipment, labor, and money to do the project. I didn't. I ended up breaking even on the contract because I couldn't get the justified change orders from the government without going to court. I wasn't going to do that again. I ended up giving the sub more money by taking it on the chin and cutting my profit to zero.

In the end, I hit some home runs financially along the way but never got the sustainable work I needed. On top of that, I was not getting the recognition the prime contractors were getting. I networked and gathered intelligence from local government contractors, learning who the players were. I needed to know who was successful and what they were doing so that I could be successful. What I learned in that time frame not only altered my company but it also put me on the map personally.

I worked with dozens of major construction companies who were getting work from the military bases along the Gulf Coast. The ones I watched closest were the 8(a) firms. These were the companies that I would have to beat. They were good at keeping their relationships close to the vest. They were especially good at keeping guys like me from kicking the door in and taking work from them. Bad mouthing unknowns was easy. And they were not shy about throwing me under the bus, especially once they realized I wanted to take away the work they had. They wanted to shut me down by convincing others I was bad juju. But I wasn't going to let that happen.

Among the 8(a) companies I was tracking, there were a few powerful firms with millions of dollars in annual revenue. I considered those companies the favorite sons and daughters of the region. I was careful not to tangle with them, and I gave them a wide berth when we crossed paths. It seemed they were untouchable, and I needed to be credible and liked to succeed. All had strong reputations. A few of the owners even had what I would call serious political connections. They had just one problem that they didn't understand. It was me. I was staying in Pensacola for their business relationships. I studied them right in front of them. I knew from my research that most of them would be graduating the 8(a) program very soon, creating a small business vacuum along the Florida panhandle. By doing my homework, I would know where to strike, as the sole-source opportunities would go to others once the favorite sons became ineligible. After all, the federal government had small business goals to meet. A few owners of these firms had already approached me to get work perceivably as a team, but I knew their offers were a ruse. They would chew me up and spit me out.

In one attempted partnership, the Sea Bee base in Mississippi offered me a post-Katrina opportunity to demolish buildings. At the time, I didn't have the bonding I needed; so I asked an 8(a) firm to work with me. As soon as the meeting with the Navy ended, the sweet old southern belle CEO told me that she would let me know what I could do on the job and that she would handle it herself. She was going to steal the project from me right in front of my face!

I couldn't believe it. She was one of those firms getting ready to leave the program, and I could tell they were getting nervous about losing work opportunities. Their clients along the Gulf Coast knew that the SBA would cut them off as well. I researched firms like hers, and I could see there was trouble on the horizon. Forced to compete on the open market, they would need another vehicle to enjoy the sole-source opportunities they hoarded for over 9 years. Why stab me in the back? It was greed, pure and simple. I played it cool, deciding that when my chance to grab a piece of the pie opened up, I would be ready. The other companies wouldn't know what hit them.

I already had established a foothold in Pensacola. I had the past performance and credibility they had as locals by working underneath them. What I needed mostly were allies. So I reached out to larger businesses operating in the target regions, staying far away from other 8(a) companies, as they were not interested in my success, just their own. I built personal relationships one handshake at a time along the Gulf Coast. To open the doors I wanted to open, I would need help. I realized I would get only one chance when the doors opened. If other companies did not buy into Sean, how could they buy into Sean's company?

I was playing a dangerous game full of risk. Having already lost a $1.5 million dollar prime opportunity by picking the wrong partner, I needed to be careful. The best way to describe my operations is flying a jet over enemy territory at night with the headlights on. If the other companies saw me as a threat, they would blow me out of the sky. How do you stop someone from shooting you down? Simple, you hide in plain sight.

So I became a very visible person to everyone down there, and I never said a word to them about what I was actually doing, not to my friends or my competition. I was that young 8(a) company everyone was trying to figure out. I would be patient. My vision for that region was out with the old and in with the new.

Finally, a request for a proposal (RFP) was released for SDVOSBs to bid an environmental contract with a US Army Corps district along the gulf coast. The major RFP was classified under the small business rules as a competitive set aside. Certain contracts issued by the government could be set aside for a specific category of business. For instance, a project could be set aside for a woman-owned, hub zone, 8(a), service-disabled veteran; or it could be unrestricted, which means anyone could bid.

This procurement came out for competition through a big district across the gulf coast USACE. A maximum not to exceed contract value of 30 million dollars over 5 years, the work was environmental compliance services throughout the southeast US foot print. This was the project I had dreamed to have.

The government wouldn't let me in the door to meet with the buyers, nor would they tell me who they were. My competitors kept mum on who they worked with, limiting access so that they could learn about me. They would introduce me only if I committed to signing agreements with them (which meant them running me around and taking as much as they could from me, like that sweet old southern belle CEO). I might as well have written them a check, because their idea of sharing was taking.

I knew that if I responded to this RFP, the people I wanted to talk to would read my background and personal information as part of the selection process. If I could not meet them, they would learn about my company through my proposal.

I had never written a proposal that big before. I needed help - and fast. By teaming up with a larger firm, I would have to share the contract work if I won. The most important thing was that I wasn't a threat. I wasn't their competition. That was the advantage of sharing the work with a larger business who understood the federal rules and regulations.

I would not have to worry about the greed. I had a company that had experience working for USACE. While I can't name the firm publicly, let's say they were the cat's meow, doing substantial work with USACE worldwide (I'll call them MEW). MEW had the recognition of the government buyers from their current contracts and their past performance. I hoped that teaming with them would bring that credibility to me. If the government saw the trust and confidence MEW had in me, maybe they would feel the same. I had a shot if MEW felt the government saw my logic.

The big thing I'd learned about working with large businesses in the past was to make sure my counterpart or large business contact has the power and authority to make contract decisions. You see, I got burnt by DC before because Buford and the PM who knew me were not empowered to make the money decisions. They were not empowered to pay me even though they knew I was owed money. They couldn't solve a problem impacting my job (like firing the 10 worthless managers or the 70 lazy workers) without getting higher approval.

Just think about going to a bank. How many vice presidents do they have? Hundreds of them, and they all have very narrow scopes of authority. The branch VP can't change your mortgage payment by negotiating terms outside set bank policies. He can do certain things, but the board ultimately controls most modern banks. They are the only ones empowered to change the policies.

In this case, my contact at MEW unequivocally had the authority to negotiate and make decisions on behalf of his firm for the proposal we were undertaking. He could make changes and commitments for the good of my company and his. That was how a true large business teaming partner should work with a small business, if you asked me. Preparing the proposal took three weeks. For the most part, the past performance presented was my own resume, because my company had limited experience. Everything I did working in the environmental field, especially my work with the Marines, went into this proposal as well. MEW added their name, resumes, and past performance to support the proposal effort. I knew there was a slim chance of success, but I had to try. Just maybe we would get noticed.

The email came a month or so later: "You are not the selected offer. We appreciate your interest. Please contact us for a debriefing." Normally, government departments let you know you had a certain number of days to request a debriefing. They didn't ask you for one.

So this was the way I read the message: "Please try again. Call us." I knew I wasn't a known entity like the winner. I could tell that something had happened behind the scenes. Something was different here, something I hadn't experienced before.

I later found out that a government official read my proposal and was completely blown away by my Marine Corps environmental experience. This person happened to be in charge of environmental project support for the Marine Corps, which included work with headquarters Marine Corps personnel that I had supported when I was an active duty Marine. The Mobile Corps was very interested in Polu Kai.

I debriefed with the contracting officer about my proposal, who told me that we had a great proposal. They could not say what position I placed as part of my debriefing. However, strong indications from the discussion had me believe we were second, without them verbally saying it. I was shocked. I had no experience with this district, and I was sure we were going to lose. But second place? No way!

After the debriefing, I thought that maybe next time Polu Kai would get a break. A week later, the phone rang. USACE requested me to meet in person. I had goose bumps. A new journey began the moment I got into the building.

Three ladies sat across the table from me. To be truthful, I only recognized one, and she had never really talked to me before. The small business deputy opened the meeting and made way for the others to speak. I came with Oscar, who had worked with the district before. He had been an 8(a) company doing work in the district prior to graduating and merging with my firm. I explained his new position, and Oscar talked about himself for a bit. The ladies knew him, but they did not pay much attention to him. They wanted to meet the jarhead. The great inquisition started. As I fielded questions from the panel, I realized what was happening.

The names of civilians in charge of cleaning up our Marine Corps bases kept popping up, most of whom I knew and who had worked with me when I was a young sergeant. I got the point; these women wanted to see if I was the real deal and if I was who I said I was. As the meeting adjourned, I stood up to say thanks and shake hands. "Nice meeting you," I told them.

The whole time, I had noticed one of the ladies not speaking, just analyzing. She looked at me and said, "I look forward to working with you." Then she turned to her small business chief. "Jane, please send PKS a sole-source request for proposal. We need them on our team." With those words, Polu Kai received our first southeast USACE contract for 3.5 million dollars. By taking second, I really took first.

When I explained to the women that I had been marketing them for over 5 years, the lady who called the shots said, "You were marketing the wrong people. When I read your proposal, I just had to meet you. I asked Jane why you were not one of our contract holders or a vendor." Then, reaching out and shaking my hand, she added in her sweet, southern voice, "Don't worry about all of that marketing stuff now. You do a good job for us, and you will have a great future."

I wanted to cry for joy! All of those years of sacrifice and hard work would finally pay off - especially the years of hard work put into the Pensacola office. You could have knocked me over with a feather. I walked out on air. And that was just the beginning. We got from that meeting three $3.5 million contracts in a row! I thought to myself, *This is coming along nicely.*

By the end of 2009, Polu Kai had our first business accolade. We were ranked 1669 in the 500-5000 list of fastest growing businesses in the country by *Inc. 500* magazine. We were really hitting our stride.

I put a lot of work into the Polu Kai ship in the early years of the business, and now we were getting new work offers almost daily. Dawn had gotten the system going, and 2010 looked like it would be a banner year. Oscar was helping to bring new talent to the construction division, and he seemed at ease with the pace.

I for one was finally going to get paid a real, sustainable wage for my work and investment. I began paying off my personal liabilities a little at a time. I also took time for a real vacation with my family. I hoped that Polu Kai could keep sailing forward into deeper waters to meet the projections I had established.

There was a lot of confidence in the company, almost too much confidence. The optimism didn't seem to bother anyone. I'll admit that it made me a little uneasy. We had built the machine, and it needed to be fed. I could attribute all the opportunity we were having to thinking big. It also had a lot to do with my unwavering persistence.

Here's another *Sean life lesson: Success is a hunger, a driving force that eats away at your soul, always searching for the keys to opening the next door. Successful people don't stand still.*

Sean P. Jensen

Part Three-

Homa

Holding On

Sean P. Jensen

Chapter 11:

The Calm Before the Storm

GROWING up in Florida, I could set my watch to the afternoon summer storms racing across the Gulf of Mexico. As I saw the cumulus clouds growing larger and dark blue in the distance, a cool wind would rush by. A breath of fresh air cut into the humidity and heat. Each day, this would happen; you knew the storms would come and pass and the still, blanketing humidity and heat would return again. That's how 2011 felt to me.

Running Polu Kai after the merger was like putting an aircraft carrier engine in a fishing boat. We had many challenges growing the group and maintaining the same dedication to success for each project. Our backlog of work kept climbing.

Part of the challenges stemmed from the need to fill key positions: for instance, the hiring of an HR person. We thought we had found our HR consultant, but she did not have the credentials and certifications she claimed. We gave her an opportunity to explain the discrepancies and provide documents to back up her resume, but she never provided the data. We had to let her go. The people that we called to check on her had never even heard of her.

We discovered her lack of professional qualifications when she told a supervisor via email not to hire a potential candidate. She claimed that he was a workman's comp risk on pain pills. The supervisor later forwarded the candidate the email, saying, "This is why you weren't hired." Her handling of this situation landed me in hot water with the Equal Employment Opportunity Commission after the candidate sued Polu Kai for discrimination. I had to pay him to settle the lawsuit, because I was responsible for my employee's actions, even if I didn't say the idiotic statement. I made changes in our hiring practices afterwards and obtained EEO insurance on Polu Kai in case another employee said something equally disastrous. Preparing for the worst is another way of taking responsibility in advance. If I had been educated on the subject, I would have taken the policy out sooner. In my opinion, you can never have too much insurance.

We searched and searched for an HR person. We had broken the 50-employee barrier in between 2010 and 2011, and we were growing exponentially. Evidence of that growth was PKS being named to the *Inc. 500* fastest-growing private company list both years, with rankings of 276 and 156 out of the 500. We seemed to be adding new people every day. We had to have a better handle on the quality and character of the people we brought into our Polu Kai family. My biggest concern was the mountain of laws and regulations we faced. My full time job seemed to be changing into chief counsel for my firm, not CEO.

After an exhaustive search, we finally found someone. She had the credentials and the references. I was ecstatic until we invited her to the Christmas party.

In my firm from the very early days, we brought everyone together for one night. Our new HR person thought that our gathering was a bad idea. She began lecturing me on how bad everyone would be. She told me how the drinking would be out of control. She claimed that she would be forced to say something because that was her job. I chuckled and told her it would be fine and that we had this party every year. I assured her that we had not ever had any problems, except some bad dancing and a little overindulgence from time to time. I told her it would be a good opportunity to interact with the team.

Hell's bells rang the magic night of the Christmas party. Our celebration was in full swing when our brand new HR rep showed up completely hammered. Apparently, she had decided to take the company credit card out to start the festivities earlier in the hotel bar. Her entrance into the Christmas party could not have been missed by the 100 or so attendees. She was wearing high heels and a dress that didn't leave much room for guessing. I knew I was going to hear about this. Before too long, I had to ask Nicole to get the HR rep out of here. As my luck would have it, she was showing Oscar how to smoke a cigar properly. You can probably imagine what that looked like. Inside, I was laughing at the insanity of the moment, but from the business side, I was saying: What a disaster!

Nicole politely asked the HR rep to leave, trying to save her from any extra humiliation. She didn't pay any attention; so a few employees carried her to her room. I had to fix this situation. Unfortunately for our new HR rep, that party would be her last company event. Some things, like finding a good HR rep, just seemed impossible during that time, but PKS kept on winning work. On the surface, nothing seemed to be going wrong, but nothing seemed to be going completely right either. We ended up hiring a consulting firm for our HR duties to save us from ourselves.

Around 2011, PKS was taking the small business world by storm. We were working in over 38 states with close to 98 employees, part-timers, and consultants. We were doing everything from sod projects to design and build construction. We cleaned up two EPA Superfund projects, multiple defense site remediation projects, and numerous demolition projects. On top of that, my firm was selected to assist in managing the construction of the BRAC 133 project, which was valued at over $1 billion for cost of construction. This project would build highly-visible 17 story towers to house the headquarters for defense agencies supporting the Pentagon and the Department of Defense. It was crazy. PKS seemed to be everywhere.

Before a storm, small things hide. So the little scurrying and splashing and humming you take for granted just ceases. Sometimes the wind stops. You drift with nothing pushing your sails. The sun calms you. Maybe you get busy repairing and improving your ship in the bright sunlight. It's a peaceful stretch of calm, but if you don't know what it means, if you aren't watching for the first gusts and the dark skies that tell you you're too far from port with a squall headed your way, you can capsize.

The whole time we were expanding and growing and sailing further and further into unknown waters, a voice in my head kept yelling at me that something wasn't right; a storm was brewing. I couldn't put my finger on what was coming. Immediately, everything showed up as a bright flash in the sky.

Three things happened in 2011 that should have brought me major concern: a run-in with the Department of the Interior followed by a congressional investigation; Oscar putting his own business first; and finally, a cure notice (a fancy word for threatening to terminate and default for failure to perform on a contract) with the VA in Florida.

Each issue had its own path to resolution that I would have to facilitate personally. While everything seemed to be running fine, these three issues distracted me throughout 2011, weakening my ability to protect the company. I would become vulnerable, and Polu Kai would take a hit.

Early in 2011, Polu Kai began a major environmental impact study for the Department of the Interior. We were supporting the draft writing of a new stream protection rule that would establish buffer zones for surface coal mining activities. My personnel experience was not that strong in the regulations we were supporting. We hired very talented experts in the field to work on the project. We also hired some of the top mining consultants in the country.

With every project in business, there is risk. When it comes to rule making and Congress, there is an important risk factor: politics. While we were working on the project, someone leaked our uncompleted draft report to the press. The report had not been accepted by the Interior Department, but it was clear that Polu Kai was going to be a political football when reports came out. Reporters and politicians leaped on the early projections to scare the public with the prospect of job losses based on our team's draft analysis of the new rule.

For starters, I am not a professional politician. But you don't have to be a politician to take political hits when the US president is calling himself the job creator and the people working for him are creating a rule that would cause job loss. Once the report leaked, congress began convening hearings (opportunities for political grandstanding and press fear-mongering), and I was getting destroyed by the client's comments. We were cured by our client. In a letter from my client, not congress, we were told to redo our report, specifically on our job loss findings.

I was trapped. If we did the work that my client, congress, demanded, we would have to pay subcontractors extra money for the rework, a few of which were billion-dollar firms. Refusing meant that the government could terminate us and then require us to pay them to hire another contractor, making us liable for all of the costs associated with the rework. One way or another, we are talking about getting stuck for millions of dollars.

When I was told, I shuddered over the consequences. Ethically, we had done everything we were asked to do, above and beyond the call of duty outlined in our contract. Now we were facing demands to change the results our experts had found. Changing results for political reasons didn't seem ethical to me.

I've hung a painting in my office, right across from reception, which depicts the famous battle of Nu'uanu Pali, where King Kamehameha the Great prosecuted his war to unite the Hawaiian Islands. Warriors from Oahu gathered on a mountain, hoping to prevent Kamehameha from passing. But the clever king found a small pass around the warriors, and using superior weapons, he pushed his enemies off the Pali cliffs through the mists to the rocks below. Like Kamehameha, I faced a determined opponent. And like Kamehameha, I would have to find a clever way around that overwhelming force.

I was not going to submit to the demands in the letter telling me that we were in default and to correct our deficiencies without a valiant effort to defend Polu Kai. This was a matter of integrity for me. We responded with as much legal force as we could muster, explaining why the Interior Department was mistaken and why it needed to pay us to do any additional work.

Up until that point in my career as a CEO, I had never received a letter threatening to terminate my firm. The situation was strange and surreal to me. You might imagine that I was as nervous as I could be, with both sides waiting for me to make the call. Then the Republican congressional committee in charge of the rule-writing investigation subpoenaed my company for every document related to the project. Unwittingly, they provided me with my clever way around the opposing force.

Fortunately for Polu Kai, we had recordings, a part of the congressional record, which told a fuller story. Transcriptions of those recordings made by my team would go to the committee unredacted. The transcriptions clearly showed that the Department of the Interior and congressional Democrats were slamming my firm without all of the facts and that certain people were ready to throw Polu Kai off a cliff. It was a hell of a pickle. Reporters were calling me up, asking for quotes about the accusations being hurled at my firm. I refused.

One thing I learned about working for the government all these years is don't bite the hand that feeds you. If you do, two things will happen. The hand will starve you (financially), or they will feed you to the wolves (government counsel). So I wasn't going to counter slander the government statements to the press now. I wanted to remain working for the government in the future. I just wanted them to do the right thing by our original contract right now.

As advised, I stayed calm. I ordered my firm to remain quiet to the press, and we set about a plan to end the situation with as little damage as possible. I took personal control over the matter. In the end, I strongly disagreed with the client's opinion as well as the Democratic congressional committee members who were hurling nasty comments about my firm to the press.

I couldn't afford to fight the government with its vast resources. And to get fully briefed on a yearlong project I'd had only administrative involvement with till now would be impossible. I decided to keep the team close and bring the all of the principals of my subs on as advisors to me and my staff. This would put all of us in the same boat to row in the same direction.

Everything we had done up to this point in business had been quiet, without incident. There was no dirt to be had on me or my firm. That was evident, because the comments directed at my business in the press were limited to the project in question, and you can bet the press would have smeared any dirt they found across the front pages.

My chief counsel was a feisty redheaded Italian whose heart was always in the right place. A George Washington Law graduate, he was the pillar I leaned on to get through those difficult months. He advised me, "Get out if you can without a fight. No small business wins in political situations like this one, caught between congress and the Interior Department. If we don't have to fight, we will win. If we do, then we will win anyways; it will just take longer." I wasn't so confident, but I was glad that he was.

The political pressure was hard for me. The press was reporting comments from the hill and others that were smearing me and my beloved Polu Kai in the press daily. The truth was so twisted by now that fighting would have taken me a PR firm and massive legal counsel to handle.

I continually cringed at disastrous, slanderous headlines: Washington Post: "Interior Department Ends Pact with Polu Kai Services;" Wall Street Journal: "Obama Admin's Proposed Rule to Block Coal Mining, Destroy Jobs;" More what.com: "Inspector General (IG): No Evidence of Political Meddling in Botched Coal Regulations;" TheHill.com: "Obama Fired Contractor That Refused To Fake Number Of Jobs Lost Due To Policies;" TheLonelyConservative.com: "Firm's Job Analysis 'Not The Basis' For End Of Mining Contract says US Official."

Thank the good Lord the smear job didn't come to that. The contracting officer for the government ruled that PKS was in the right and that the government could not terminate us without just cause. Nor could they make us do more work without compensation. Obama didn't fire me! As you can see, politics was not for the weak of heart.

Since there was no cause and no wrongdoing on our part, I decided to opt out of a contract extension after discussing with the client, following my lawyer's advice in an effort to save my house of cards. Giving up the contract was a bitter pill to swallow, because we couldn't finish the report without receiving fire from all sides. We were both vilified and praised in the press, all of which will forever remain on Google. On the other side of the fence, this contract was clearly a no-win situation.

No matter what we wrote, the politicians were running each other over about the job losses. What we produced was technically an incomplete draft because the government never accepted it.

In time to come, more articles and an IG investigation would completely clear my company's name. If you were to ask me to write another government report that impacts rule-making, you might get a funny look.

Interestingly enough, the IG from (our client) the Department of the Interior didn't find any wrongdoing with the Office of Surface Mining, Interior Department, either. They released that report 5 days before Christmas in 2013. It was a slow news day, which was pretty convenient, if you ask me.

Here's another *Sean life lesson: Think hard before you jump into a government, rule-making contract.* Even if it is just a draft document and you have all of the right players on your team, you can still suffer.

In my humble opinion, you will somehow inevitably turn into a political football and end up pissing off one side or the other. When it comes to making rules and regulations, someone out there won't like the policy.

[Side note: It is now 2015, and the full draft report still hasn't been released. Even the new contractor still hadn't put anything together yet. Go figure. It is probably a lot more serious than anything my company or my subs were doing, and I am sure it is not over, either. There went four months of my life that I will never get back! I am glad to be out of it - lesson learned.]

About the time I finished that mess, new storm clouds were rising around PKS. One in particular was right down the road from my office in Tampa. We got the second letter of the year stating that the government was going to default us if we didn't fix the HVAC units we installed at a VA hospital we were under contract with.

Oscar was right there in Tampa. He was doing everything he could to solve the problem, as a partner should. But I decided to attend personally to this storm. The distractions were backing up. As I began to work on the issue, I felt that Polu Kai was missing leadership in Florida.

Clearly, this was an easy fix. We needed to replace the units.

More legal action would be required, but not against the government this time. The manufacturer of the equipment had clearly sold us lemons. The government was right. The units were leaking. They were horribly constructed. I threatened to sue the subcontractor's bond and told them they would have to replace the units at their cost. Unfortunately, the government had given us too many chances to fix the units installed when they should have been rejected by everyone, including my personnel. This lapse would cause a major distraction for me. I noted to myself during this event that where there is smoke, there is fire. We were not holding the high standards of construction I preached every day.

Late in 2011, some underlying issues and concerns with Oscar began to rise to the surface. He was the project executive both on the draft study turned political football and the executive in charge of the region where the HVAC unit project was located. What was going on? Was he losing focus? Why didn't he see these problems like I did? He was a licensed general contractor! He should have seen the problem before the government did and proposed a fix.

When Oscar bought into my company, he agreed to wind down his business. I told him that I wanted his undivided attention during his tenure with PKS. But from the time he joined PKS in 2008, Oscar seemed to be constantly getting projects with his old business that had to be done and telling me that he had to perform because of contractual commitments. I didn't question his word. I even offered PKS employees to support the winding down of his business operation where necessary. We had an agreement to that effect.

For the most part, I believe that Oscar was being truthful, most of the time. But another part of me knew that not all alliances were good business. Even the great George Washington said, "Beware of entangling alliances," in his farewell address to the nation. He knew that other nations would look out primarily for their own interests, not ours. A 32-degree Master Mason myself, I took that statement seriously. A man would look out for his own business before his partner's business.

Deep down, I began to worry that Oscar was not focused on PKS business. Adding friendly pressure, I began to comment to him that he needed to wrap his old business stuff up. After all, PKS had previously been protested on a couple of contract wins, the protestor accusing me of being affiliated with Oscar's firm. That was never the case.

After much government scrutiny and inspections of my firm, the government also agreed that was not the case. But Oscar's business was a fouled anchor dragging on the Polu Kai ship.

To further my concerns, a few construction projects in Florida were having major issues that Oscar was not addressing, like the one with the HVAC units. These issues began to flare up and take a considerable amount of time, almost half of 2011.

During an office visit, I found out that a couple of my important personnel were tied up working on Oscar's old business projects. Addressing his projects and problems was weakening my own business performance. Tensions ran high after the two previous incidents, and Oscar's excuses kept coming. If you asked me, I'd say that greed had set in. I got the feeling that Oscar was not going to give up his business at all. I just wanted him to man up and be honest about it. I had to put a stop to this nonsense.

The last straw came at a construction meeting with my senior staff members. We were reviewing projects and going over subcontractor bids for projects that we were working on. I asked for copies of sub proposals. The room fell silent, and I knew that something was afoot. When I got the proposal for a demo on a project we just received, it had Oscar's company's name on it. I flipped out. The estimator for my firm said that was the only bid he could get. This employee came over in the merger with Oscar, and I knew he had no loyalty to me. No matter the consequence, I told Oscar privately that it was time for him to go.

If he wasn't going to man up, I would. I had finally hit the breaking point with him. I had known for months that his divided loyalty was an issue. If there weren't so many issues he was handling on our behalf, I would have probably moved on sooner. Oscar knew that he didn't really want to be around any post-8(a) company when the SBA advantage was gone. Nobody did. In 2011, 2013 seemed very close, and he thought it was time for him to collect on his little investment.

For me, our partnership dissolution centered on a lack of trust. Once trust was broken, I knew it couldn't be repaired. Like most US Marines, I was loyal to a fault until I saw betrayal. I did not believe that Oscar had the PKS business or my best interest at heart. His decision-making processes had made his interests clear. My partner had become a liability.

After months of legal wrangling and posturing and threats, we settled on a buyout agreement, and Oscar moved on. At the time of his departure, I offered everyone currently working around him an opportunity to leave and join him if they wanted to. A few took the offer. There were a few bad seeds that didn't leave, and I would have to deal with them in time. Their loyalties had been compromised during the recent months' events.

For me, the bonds of trust and loyalty are critical to running a business. Without them, you're looking at business suicide. Crooks have to work ten times harder than men of integrity. I always honor my agreements, even when doing so hurts. You will have to kill me to stop me from doing the right thing.

With Oscar, the disagreements became too personal. I believe the issue was truly with him and no one else. "Let's just see how far I can push it with Sean," he seemed to think. He found a place to work during the height of the economic recession so that he could keep his own company going and pay the mortgage on his building at the same time, as I agreed to do when he came on.

I paid the lease on his building every month. And that payment bothered me. Oscar was making a killing on me, but I never said a word. I was his number one client, for all intents and purposes. Keep in mind, we were averaging $28 million dollars a year for the last 3 years at this time. We were successful. And when he was working with my best intentions, I was thankful. That was the agreement. I always treated him as an equal, even though I had full, unequivocal control of the firm. Somehow, I never felt the reciprocation of respect from him. Others below me lamented how Oscar seemed to take advantage of PKS.

The divorce was over. Now Polu Kai had to heal. That would take time. And 2011 would be a rough year. Little did I know that it would also be the last year we would make a profit for some time.

Here's another *Sean life lesson: Don't be envious of other people's success. You shouldn't mind anyone making honest money.* To be successful, an agreement has to be honored by both sides. And in matters of distrust, perception is most often reality.

I enjoy watching the effects of people making money. In fact, my favorite time of year is Christmas, when I can spread the wealth of my profits with the employees that have helped create it. I think that if you work hard and you perform a job well, you're entitled to make a profit. Bonuses should honor the hard work and acknowledge the success of the whole crew. I have always worked with my subs and business partners to do just that. Sometimes I've been blind to what the other person's intentions were. Not every marriage is perfect.

Chapter 12:

Creatures of the Deep

Sean P. Jensen

POLU Kai was a big company that covered a large foot print. But we were nowhere near as big as the agencies we served. Working with the government was something like sailing in deep waters. Huge creatures of the deep needed our ship, but they were too big to see our best interests. They were huge. They swam to the deepest parts of the ocean. They had concerns I didn't share, because we were at such different levels of size. I had seen in my struggles with congress that sailing too near them when they wanted to go in a different direction could rock my ship in a drastic way. But I also knew that those huge creatures of the deep and I needed one another. My next huge challenge would involve keeping the behemoth government and myself in a good working relationship, despite the danger to my ship.

I also knew that with Polu Kai's footprint spreading across the United States and engaging more and more employees. I would need to find a new leader to help me. Oscar had left a deficit in leadership behind him. I set out on the task of filling that deficit right away.

2012 marked the tenth anniversary of my company, and it marked a turning point for me. Once again, I was forced to rely on myself, without business partners. There is something dangerous and exciting about standing alone as the sole responsible person for the success or failure of a business. It's like standing at the prow of a mighty ship with the waves close below you and the ocean spray in your face as you cut into mighty swells. In this case, I felt capable and experienced enough to manage the Polu Kai ship. After all, ten years of running and growing a multi-million-dollar company was a pretty strong resume. I was battle tested.

Every now and then, I would wonder to myself: *Can I pull this off?* Then I would say to myself: *Yes! You can do anything, Sean. Just look at where you have been and where you are now!*

I took assessment of my company's position. The paper looked good. The audited financials told a good story. We had $17 million in new work, an active backlog for any business. We had $1.6 million cash on hand and an open credit line of another million dollars available. We were in a very solid position starting 2012 in regards to equity and cash. We were in good standing with every vendor. I will tell you; the separation from Oscar hurt. But it could have been a lot worse had I decided to go the legal route. Now his payoff was the equivalent to paying a ghost executive for the next five years. I could handle that drain.

Considering that I hadn't quite finished paying off my first partner, Harry, I knew I would have to work hard to keep on course now. Thanks to some great planning, Polu Kai had some substantial competitive wins in 2011. We won a $100,000,000, 5-year limited competition contract in Florida. In late November, we won our first of 2 task orders on a $49,000,000, 5-year limited competition contract in Hawaii.

Work was underway in Hawaii. We held firm in our western division in Denver, Colorado. Everything seemed normal. In fact, we decided to celebrate our 10-year anniversary with a little luau across the street from our headquarters. In October of 2011, we even hired a new executive vice president to fill the leadership gap Oscar had left. Don was a retired military officer who seemed to be a great fit to lead the many veterans in my firm, both civilian and prior service. I had a good feeling that his impact would be positive, and I engaged him.

2012 would be the big, final push for us in the 8(a) program. It was crunch time. Sales were up to me and Randy, my Cuban ambassador. Knowing that we were going to graduate soon, Gail left the company. I would have liked her to stay, but without the 8(a) program, she couldn't use her true value and connections fully. She had served her purpose in helping us grow, and for that I will always be thankful. Like a few of the other senior managers, Gail wanted to get off the train and cash out. She left, along with the estimator who had defended Oscar on that sub bid. Lucky for me, I could handle the loss, and I dutifully paid them off.

As I predicted, and as I planned three years ago, the transition from minority business to street competitor was happening. I felt good. Spring 2012 came, and Polu Kai celebrated the last 10 years. For me, having survived so many battles was a great feeling. The success we had known as a start-up business was awe inspiring. Other young companies looked up to us. We were that crazy Hawaiian jarhead firm that had great people and did great work. I felt like a proud dad!

But I didn't get too carried away. We weren't out of the woods yet. I also knew that outside pressures were strong, seeing that much of our work centered on the Defense Department. "Sequestration" and "Obama Care," words I would like to forget, were going to take a toll on Polu Kai. The Supreme Court ruling on health care came through, and our business was hit hard. We endured a massive increase in insurance costs just with the passage of the law! Our insurance rates went up as soon as the law passed and every year after that. Unfortunately for my employees, I had to pass on some of those increases and change our health insurance plans. Up until then, we had paid 100% for a single employee and a very high percent on covered families.

It was crazy. I talked to the firm collectively and explained the burden of the new law. My employees, my extended family, took the hit in stride, and we got through. "Bad for business but good for everyone," I was told.

Healthcare used to be a good leverage to retain talent among small businesses. That industry edge is now gone. While some employees used to come to a smaller company because of the great benefits, because healthcare costs were so high, now we are all in the same boat.

The summer storm season would soon begin, and I don't mean hurricanes that would supply us with blue-roof work. This storm started, of all places, back in Florida. This time the tropical wave was centered on PKS. From there, it moved like a major hurricane rolling up the east coast toward me and the headquarters in Virginia.

At first, the information we got about this coming storm was sketchy, like a line of squalls. Back in October of 2010, we had started a major fire alarm project for the VA and the US Army Corps. The work was simple enough and straightforward: demolish the old system and install the new. The government had enough money to do one of four buildings at the VA Hospital in West Palm. We negotiated a contract in 2010 to do just that: to replace the system in the main building only. The other buildings would follow in future contracts, as funding became available. My team in Florida, headed by Oscar, was confident that we would finish early.

Up until the end of 2011, everything was moving fine. We had some issues. The Department of Labor (DOL) came in October of 2011 and audited the employee payrolls made by my subcontractor to its employees. I thought: *We are almost done with the project; so why worry?* I was told we were near completion, and the invoicing and payments reflected what the team told me.

Then the VA came in trumping USACE and rejecting our work performed on the top floors of the main hospital. They provided a huge punch list. I was, of course, confused. So much of the job was complete, and payments had been made to our subcontractors. We had been paid for the work.

What was going on? We were scheduled to finish in March of 2012.

We were at 80% complete on a $3.2 million project. *This is crazy,* I thought. I felt that the DOL issues could be handled by forcing the subcontractor to pay the employees. The sub had provided a performance and payment bond form of insurance security. I would hold them to their bond, or so I thought.

I sent Don, my new executive vice president (EVP) to look into the situation. When he got there, he told me that the subcontractor on the job was struggling. The DOL had really turned the project upside down when they started their investigation. There would be money to pay out of the subcontractor's pocket because of underpayments to his employees. The final tally would remain unknown for some time to come. But the sub's performance and payment bond on the project was his personal guarantee that we could collect from the bonding company if we had to sue. At least, that is what we thought.

The subcontractor's bonding company was put on notice about the DOL problems with the sub and the VA's problems with his work, and we asked them to remedy the situation. We did what any prudent contractor would do and started planning for the worst. We needed to know how we would complete the work with a new subcontractor if this one failed. I charged Don and the trusted VP of finance, Dawn, to show me the options. I began tracking the project remotely on a daily basis. But for now, I had to let my executives sort this problem out.

Remember what I said about creatures of the deep? Any huge creature inevitably collects parasites, and some of them, like sharp barnacles, can cut you as you get near them. Some government officials that make life difficult for small companies are like that. They don't reflect the intent or the character of the government. But they're stuck in place, and they don't really care if they take some of your hide off or knock holes in your ship.

At the same time that we faced problems with our subcontractor on the VA hospital, a barnacle was scraping our hull. By the summer of 2012, another project in Tampa was taking a hit from a contracting officer who would not take meetings to discuss changes to a project. Instead, we were getting cure emails and threats of termination because we didn't know what we were doing, or so we were told. My review of the project said that we were in trouble if we didn't get on the record and take some action. Of course, none of the crap being thrown at us by said government official was true; nevertheless, PKS had to expend more time, effort, and money to complete the work. I added that project to Don's list of things to do, as other issues that required my attention started popping up in Virginia.

Any good contractor will tell you that the death of a project starts with rework, going back and doing the same task twice. In most cases, rework is minor. It is not uncommon in the industry. Usually, you will have been paid by then, and you have to fix the repairs out of pocket. Small punch lists are not unusual. But left unchecked, they can quickly rise out of control.

The HVAC units I mentioned before were a case in point. Had everyone acted sooner, we would not have had the issue in the first place. That neglect cost me time and money.

The other major threat to a contractor is passing the contract completion date. In those cases, delays to the project created by untimely performance, client delay, weather, or other factors create additional unplanned cost. It can affect the government, but most of the time the prime contractor bears the burden. Most contracts have a margin of error built into the estimate. These days, it's a slim dollar amount if you want to win work.

I mentioned issues requiring my attention in Virginia and keeping me from really digging into supervising the projects in Tampa I'd left to Dawn and Don. During 2012, two additional capital projects in my mid-Atlantic region were in danger of losing major dollars. One was a year past due because of changes to the scope and work. The government owed us change orders. Instead, they sat on them for what seemed like an eternity. We were working on a high-profile historical renovation project, the project to restore Grant Hall, commonly referred to as the "Lincoln Court House." It's where Mary Surratt and the other Lincoln assassination conspirators were tried and hanged. No low-profile projects for Polu Kai!

The other project was near and dear to my heart. We were restoring the Smedley D. Butler Stadium at my alma mater, Quantico Marine Corps Base. An historic stadium, built by hand by Marines after World War I, the original construction was commissioned by none other than two-time Medal of Honor winner General Smedley D. Butler. He was a legend in the Marines. At the time of his death in 1940, he was the most decorated Marine in US history. The Navy decided that the only common sense thing to do was award the reconstruction renovation project to a US Marine-owned business (me), seeing that the Marines Corps itself was out of the stadium-building business. Total construction for all of the work totaled $5.7 million: a major project for me and my firm.

I knew we could do it. Artificial turf, new bleachers, and repair to the field were all additional work made necessary by ground hogs undermining the hill structure on which the stadium was built. Everything was going right, but nothing seemed to be going right. The project had major contract and personnel issues that had to be addressed it seemed daily. Even so, I was determined to complete the tasks at hand.

Then whammo! The SBA sent me a letter telling me I was suspended from the 8(a) program because I missed my non-small business revenue goals by a few percentage points.

In short, all of the work you do while you're an 8(a) participant has revenue percentage goals you have to meet each year you are in the program. A percentage of that work has to be outside of the 8(a) program. This ideally will help you grow other avenues of business to sustain you once you graduate from the program.

Not meeting the goals was an understatement in reality: we blew them away. There was little funding, and sequestration was setting upon our non-8(a) federal work. But the blows kept coming. We needed new projects more than anything, because we were in our final year of the program when we really expected to knock our last year in the program out of the park.

I wrote a letter to the SBA explaining why we didn't meet our goals and how tough economic times were. The bad news was still everywhere about the Great Recession. I showed them that we had in fact won large, non-8(a) contracts in Florida and in Hawaii. The task orders or contracts had not been released or started due to no fault of ours. Based on the information I provided them, they rescinded their determination, thus clearing the way for me to continue to sell. That decision bought me time to make my final sales push as an 8(a). But those creatures of the deep just kept rocking my boat.

Back to West Palm: by now Dawn and Don had provided me with a plan. They attached the best-case scenario, worst-case scenario, and the scenario leading down the middle of the road. All of them were ugly. The number I stared at the most was the worst. It was like being hit by two metro buses. $800,000 kept staring back at me. That number was the price to fix the project with another subcontractor and complete the task. I thought to myself:

How did we get here? There was more.

The current subcontractor was slowing down performance, complaining about cash flow and payments. He released all of the temporary workers he had on the job, fearful they would revolt some more. Clearly, some disgruntled individual had called the DOL on him. By now, he had spent the $800,000 bucks he had already been paid. Any profit I was going to make on the job was going to be gone.

Even with all of the bad news, Don and the rest of the management team believed that we could pull through. I had to prepare myself for the worst case and the fact that we were not going to make a dime in profit that year as a company. This was a prime example of *Sean life lesson: Prepare and expect the worst, but strive for the best.*

The news came that the DOL wanted my subcontractor to back pay $465,000 to its employees, dutifully telling me that if he didn't pay, I would be responsible. Adding that figure to the $800,000 worst-case scenario, my number would climb to over $1 million dollars in losses on the West Palm Beach project, if that projected worst-case scenario happened, too.

What occurred next was almost impossible to fathom. As I live and breathe, I had not imagined it, but it happened. The bonding company that guaranteed the insurance paper on my violating subcontractor went bankrupt. Almost as soon as that happened, my subcontractor walked off the job and declared bankruptcy to avoid a lawsuit from me.

Heartbroken, trembling inside, and full of anger and rage, I looked at my team. Beyond the worst case had happened, and now I was the last man standing. I would be held responsible without any security. The sub had walked away, just up and quit. Why stay if there was no gun to his head? I obviously was not going to pay him any more money on work he wouldn't fix. I had done everything I could to get this guy through to the end, even forking over additional payments as a show of good faith and commitment on a recommendation from Don.

Now I was in trouble for real. I would have to hire a new subcontractor, or I was in danger of being fired. I had not received a cure or a threat from the government on this job yet, but I just knew they were waiting to see how I was going to react.

If I chose badly, one flick of that behemoth tail would mean the end for my company. I took a step back and did what I had to do. I took responsibility and hired a union electrical company to do the work right and complete the project.

I prepared for the worst. Here is where my ADD in High Definition paid off. With so many things happening at the same time, I felt like I was back on a major chemical spill making 5-second decisions every minute of the day. I called a meeting with the executives, and I listened to all of the problems at hand. I needed to know how bad everything really was. "Don't sugarcoat the issues. Let me know if you're concerned about a project." The luau was over, and I knew it.

There is something called contractual duty to proceed in the federal contract world. Even if you think the government is wrong on a contract-related issue, they can direct you to proceed with the work. My lawyer always tells me, "If you keep working, the government can't just fire you." The caveat is that you have to be making positive progress. Only in the rarest circumstance can a company walk off the job.

I had watched other companies walk off projects in the past, and I knew that decision never went well for them. Nine times out of ten, they were found responsible and ordered to pay back the government for their losses and contract procurement costs. Even if a company was in the right, that money would most surely come out of its hide.

You see, the bonding companies provide the insurance bond guarantee to the government and charge the construction company a nice fee. And the owner has to provide a personal guarantee to the bonding company tied to all of his personal assets called a personal indemnity agreement. You sign this agreement with the insurance firm or brokerage. I, of course, have one of those. The cost of whatever damage the client may be awarded will be your financial responsibility in the end, when the insurance company leverages upon you the indemnity you signed. Contractually, when you make a deal with the government, you have to complete the project or lose everything you have.

"Finish the work - that's just what we are going to do on every project in trouble!" I said. My executive team went into the field to give me a full assessment. Operations managers took over as project managers on the worst projects or assisted if they found competent leadership in place. If a project wasn't sinking below the waves, we were going to leave it alone. I knew we were going to hit rock bottom, but I didn't know how far we had to fall.

I needed an assessment to see how much more those government leviathans were going to rock my ship.

Sean P Jensen

Chapter 13:

Taking the Helm

Sean P Jensen

A captain can't man the helm of his ship every minute of every day. Besides attending to purely human needs like food and sleep, a captain must chart the course of the ship, record progress in the ship's log, and keep the crew ship-shape. He relies on competent officers to steer the ship while he completes his other duties. But when there's a storm or an attack or an accident, a good captain takes the helm and stays there until the danger passes.

Because Polu Kai sailed dangerous waters that needed immediate action from me, I took the helm and put an interim plan into action, something that would even our keel. I would use Polu Kai's credit line to fund the repairs and completion of the West Palm project. Any profit we'd expected there would be lost.

The profit we made on the good jobs we would divert to meet the requirements of the problem projects. Don would take on the West Palm oversight in conjunction with Randy. My southeast operations manager would take on the Tampa project personally, with support of a new PM.

I would work with Aaron, my mid-Atlantic VP, to handle the northern problem projects: Quantico and Grant Hall. I would be part of the process on all of the projects, receiving daily updates from all parties involved with each project. Meanwhile, I would personally push the sales to make sure we didn't lose momentum. New work was the only way I knew how to pay off these debts.

I started making phone calls to my banker and bonding agent, advising them that we were going to take a hit. "This is no ordinary hit," I warned them. Our very survival was at stake. My goal would be to break even for the year, if possible. A few people questioned my judgment on the notifications I made. I didn't blink. If I was an investor in your company, I would want to know if you were going to get killed. Besides, if they weren't going to support me, I wanted to know then and not 6 months later with them asking, "Why didn't you tell us?" They needed to know.

Simple enough, right? Well, not so much. We weren't doomed yet, but the reality was clear. We were going to lose lots of money. Remember, I mentioned that we had backlog and that we were still working on other projects. That work would help, but it wouldn't be enough.

Maxing the credit line and making minimum monthly payments was dangerous. It would send red flags to the bank, with whom we had an excellent nine-year track record. I had great flexibility to make decisions on money, projects, and bonding requirements. I still had control. No one really said no. I had earned the trust from the outside vendors to engage almost any opportunity within our range. That power would all be taken out of my hands in time with a major financial loss. It was a matter of when, not if.

Don struggled with the constant hits. He wanted to help; so he kept some of the government officials off my back to give me time. Everyone was getting hit from all directions. I told him that we had to press on. I remember his words to me when we were standing in his office in early October 2012. Having just reviewed the West Palm projections again for 200th time, we knew that the $800,000 worst case scenario for West Palm wasn't even close. The project was now a projected $1.2 million loss, with the worst case scenario expecting to crest at $1.8 million to fix the project. *Holy shit!* I thought to myself as I absorbed that figure.

Standing next to Dawn, Don looked at me and said, "I don't know what else to do for you, Sean. These are big issues. It's your future. You're going to have to lead us out of this. This is the worst thing I've had to deal with."

I hadn't personally been to the project. Instead, I had been relying on him and three others for my updates. With so many huge waves coming at me, I couldn't be everywhere. I was crushed inside, but Don's statement was just the motivation I needed to get to the site. Even Dawn, my secret weapon, didn't have an answer for this disaster. After all, she was just trying to keep the bills paid every day.

Sometime after the meeting, Don became ill, probably because of the stress. He had a heart condition, the last thing you want to have in our business. He told me that I would write about this crisis someday, and then I could lecture college business classes. As he had told me, I would have to lead Polu Kai out of the rough seas. He had faith in me.

The last months of 2012 had to end with a real plan. The interim plan wasn't going to work because of the magnitude of losses. We were still bleeding, and the bad news kept coming.

Another two projects, both in Hawaii, were getting ready to implode because of contract disputes with the government. I was thinking to myself: *You've got to be kidding me!* One was easily fixable, while the other one was a nightmare waiting to happen. I can't go into great detail; litigation still exists today. Suffice it to say that things were going to get ugly.

I went out to Honolulu before Thanksgiving, I saw what needed to be done on the fixable project, and directed every component of the project to get it completed. I would spare no expense to complete the fixable project before Christmas.

After all, when I went into the office to meet the client, he told me that he planned on firing me and had a letter ready for me. With intensity and confidence, I told him, "Put that letter back in the drawer." I reminded him that he had contributed to the faltering of this project and that his team was holding information we needed to complete the job. I knew that going into the meeting because I'd read up on the entire project on the way over to the island.

I explained to the client that it would be better if he put his letter away and allowed us to complete the project. Given the small size of the project, litigation was not worthwhile. I would pay for the changes, and he would give me the time extension so that there would be no default.

He put the letter away. We got the government changes to the design, and we built what needed to be built - not without a couple of sea-monster tussles first. At least something would get done in 2012. I'd achieved a small win, but it was one less distraction.

Somehow, through all of this negotiation, I remembered a saying from Marine combat training that had to do with treatment of combat wounds. "Stop the bleeding; start the breathing; protect the wound; treat for shock." These words were a mantra in training. They were embedded in every Marine's memory during combat first aid. I applied them in my plan. I started communicating with my key advisors on a level I don't think they had ever experienced. I also opened direct lines of communication between me and the field project managers and superintendents. I had communicated with them before, but never like this. Who would give me the direct skinny on day to day operations? The people on the front lines, that's who. Some of these folks would only talk with me several times a year. Now they would talk to me daily. I had the helm, all right. And I was gripping it for dear life.

Sean P. Jensen

Chapter 14

Down to the Waterline

Sean P. Jensen

WHEN a ship burns, not all of it burns. The fire consumes the wood to the waterline, where the waves quench it and claim the hull. Even a badly burned ship will have an intact keel – the strongest part of the ship - running stem to stern. If you have the will and the resources, you can raise the keel and rebuild everything that the fire consumed. It's work, but if you love the ship, you'll do the work.

For me, I knew in October 2012 that Polu Kai was going to have to burn to the waterline first in order to raise the keel and start again. The fire burning us was too hot. There was no restructuring or chapter 7 to protect me from creditors. We were too small for that. I knew that in 2013, the creditors would all come knocking my door. *It will be all or nothing,* I told myself.

My initial conversations with the bank were interesting. They did not react at all. "Best keep this to yourself," was the message I got. The VP of the bank, who vouched for our $1,000,000 revolving line of credit, told me I would be fine until the Polu Kai financial statement came out. He wasn't in that department anymore; so I would be assigned a new banker, who would work with me. *Talk about running for the hills,* I thought. I didn't blame him, but I had to allow myself an internal *Wow!* at his departure from our relationship.

On the other hand, the bonding agent, whom I considered a close friend and ally, chose to warn the insurance company, preparing them for the worst. Scott was the owner of a burgeoning brokerage. Bonds were his only mantra. I had met him back in 2008. At the time, I told him that he could have a crack at my business if my relationship with my bonding company at the time ever crumbled. I liked him a lot, and his feisty Philadelphia, PA attitude was a charmer for me. So when AIG failed and pulled all of my bid bonds in 2009, I called Scott. He stepped up and bonded every project I had won, thus saving my butt from the government, which requires companies to deliver bonds 10 days after the award of a bonded contract.

Over the years, Scott and I built a strong relationship. I helped him with his business, and he helped me with mine. That's how relationships should work. I was worried for him and me. I knew that if I failed, his young company would most likely fail, too. After all, I was one of his top premium clients. My potential doom worried him, too.

But all he wanted to know was if there were any changes. I told him no, but we were not sure how bad the loss would be until the numbers came in.

Scott talked to the guy in charge of underwriting for the bonding company. "I am going to feel him out," he told me. I knew the underwriter, who was a retired US Army sergeant major and a great guy. We ribbed each other about the service branches we represented. He liked me, even if I was a Marine and not Army. In this case, he relied on the word of a Marine and recommended to his leadership to continue bonding Polu Kai. This support meant that his job was at stake now, too.

The sergeant major and Scott were excellent allies. They were the two people outside of my organization, besides my wife, who believed I could turn Polu Kai around.

I am glad that they backed me, because we had managed to refill our back log, winning an additional $16 million in new work. I was hopeful and barely optimistic. Please don't be wowed by that figure. I ran into a new scenario. On every new bonded project, there would be funds control. When we were paid on a project, the bonding company would take the money from us and hold it in escrow.

The money earned could only be spent on that project. On funds control jobs, profits could rarely be taken because the funds control management company's job was to keep as much of the money as possible as collateral insurance until completion. On top of that, the company paid an additional fee for the funds control company to manage that money, another percentage point. All those wins did was to keep us working.

Looking at the bright side, we were still creating opportunity. If we were creating opportunity, we were succeeding. Though the ship was still on fire, the flames were cooling and leaving a strong keel untouched. Only every now and then would there be a flare up.

One flare up included one of the newest projects won in September of 2012. The estimator, the review team, and I all missed a key testing item that would cost an additional $300,000 not estimated in our original quote. Before we started the project or got into 2013, we were going to have to take another hit. I mean, coming to work was like living a Greek tragedy. I was thinking: *How in Hell do I explain that snafu to the funds control company?*

Christmas of 2012 was a brief respite from the world. While I worked to clean up the one fixable Hawaii project, Polu Kai had its annual company Christmas party. Though I'd thought about canceling, I had already paid a non-refundable fee for the venue in July. By the end of November, all of the travel had been booked. I must have been a sight: the blood slowly draining from my veins, my tenuous smile short, and my mind racing with issues. I did my best to keep up my appearance and show no fear. I was just getting 4-5 hours of sleep at night, if I was lucky.

Don, who had become ill after the $800,000 worst case scenario for West Palm increased so drastically, resigned in February 2013 due to medical issues. I really did like him and still speak highly of him today. If there was any upside to his retirement at all, his leaving cleared the way for me to do what I did best and rely on myself as I had in the past.

This time was a little different. I had allies, some with a stake in my business like Scott and the sergeant major. But they had nowhere near what I had to lose: my job, my house, my daughter's college tuition, and my future in life. No one would touch a person who failed like this. I also was thinking about my employees and their families, who depended on me.

The vendors, many of whom had been with me for years, trusted me to honor my commitments. Where would I find an extra million dollars to pay for the rework at West Palm? So much was happening. I felt like a punching bag. I would solve a problem, and three more would pop up.

For instance, I resolved the subcontractor DOL matter with a settlement in October 2012 by paying over $135,000 on behalf of the bankrupt subcontractor and the bonding company. Then two days after Christmas, the DOL sent a letter demanding me to pay more money because their calculations were incorrect. The letter didn't arrive until January 2013.

They demanded that I pay an additional $300,000. The settlement agreement was not in writing. I was told, "Pay up, or we're going to take the money we are holding!" *My God!* I asked myself: *Is there any break in the storm clouds?* At this point, it was nearly the worst year of my life.

January of 2013 would be no different than January of any other year, except for the fact that it was the last month I would be in the 8(a) program. Somehow, some way, Polu Kai had managed to internalize last year's problems and protect our biggest asset: our SBA status.

We received our last 8(a) award on February 13, 2013, the day of my graduation. With little fanfare, I signed the contract for $700,000 to clean up a Coast Guard facility in Florida. I called the SBA rep, thanked her for her work with us, and told her that I appreciated the SBA's effort in helping small businesses like us. I asked her if the SBA would be sending me a certificate of graduation. The reply from SBA was, "We don't do that anymore." I quipped to myself: *It must be government cutbacks.* After all, sequestration was around the corner.

Since I am talking about everything, I will say this. The SBA 8(a) program, if done right, can be a major catapult to success. If I write another book, that program may very well be the topic. I am glad to be out of the program, because the paperwork and government reporting are an enormous weight to bear. The amount of personal information and detail you must provide to them while you're in the program would make anyone cringe. In my office, I have an entire wall of reports and binders and documents, all dedicated to that 9-year program. Graduating was the end of one journey and the beginning of a new one.

I just had to wait for the flames to die so that I could raise my keel and rebuild my ship.

Part Four-

Ho'oponopono

Setting Things Right

Sean P. Jensen

Chapter 15:

The Tide Turns

ANY sailor knows that you can't fight the tide. If you try, you'll spend a lot of effort going nowhere fast. No – a good sailor waits until the ocean beckons his ship to fly from port, until the sea carries him willingly, until the tide turns and takes him away.

It wouldn't be long, and the tide would start turning for Polu Kai. Late in 2012, at my direction we started a complete review of every employee at Polu Kai. Not telling the executives exactly what I had in mind, I asked them to rate every employee they had in their department. Once completed, I personally reviewed every rating and began my strategic planning. This had to be done because of all the fires that were burning at the time. I would need this as part of my survival preparation. By February 2013, we knew how bad our losses were going to be. The auditors and accountants had come and gone. The news would be enough for one person to say to me, "Sean, I just want to curl up like a baby in a corner and cry."

I knew he was kidding, but his emphasis on how bad things had gotten was clear. The flames had consumed all the wood they would take and met the waterline. We had burnt to the ground and felt our keel shake the seabed. We had hit bottom.

We financially reported a net loss of $2,100,000. My equity in the company that previously had exceeded $1 million was gone. A $3,000,000 loss in one year made my new equity negative $1.8 million. I seemed to owe everybody. Worse, paying off the two ex-partners far exceeded anything I had saved over the years. One of them was almost completely paid off, while the other was just starting. I was not dumbfounded. I was in shock.

Not too long after that revelation, the bonding company made the decision to cut me off. They would control whether or not I bid a bonded job. There would be strict underwriting, and I was given quiet instructions from Scott and the sergeant major not to press my luck. Only emergency bonds would be issued to me with funds control. Essentially, the gift I received from them, bonding us in 2012, was just that: a gift. No way would the underwriters sign off now without leadership's direct approval in 2013.

The word was out for all to see in the insurance world. They, too, had been hit by the First Sealord Bonding Company bankruptcy; many small businesses had. It was the equivalent of a mini-AIG bailout, even though there was no bailout. The commonwealth of PA took over the now-defunct bonding company. You would be lucky to get pennies on the dollar if you got anything at all from a bankrupt company. Multiple people in the know told me, "Forget it, Sean. You are screwed!"

I was called to Pennsylvania to meet with the leadership of the bonding company backing my firm. They asked me point blank if I could save the company. It was a hard meeting. I had prepared a plan and was prepared to present it. I told them I could save the company.

The leadership looked at me and said, "Fine." They didn't even want to see the plan, "You can email us later." One executive said, "Do not drop him. Let his company work."

Other executive bean counters in the room privately wanted me out. I never really asked who made the call to save me. I assumed that the sergeant major had something to do with it. The leadership had been politicking for my removal before I went up there. Writing bonds to a failing firm just wasn't done. Leadership was with me for now, but I needed to prove myself.

What people don't know is that when you sign your personal indemnity (life) over to an insurance company, you give them the right to protect their interests. If they think you're incompetent, they can take over your projects to protect themselves, and you have to pay them to do it. It is very serious business.

At this time, I had over $25,000,000 in active projects at various stages. There could be new losses that had not yet been realized. I was lucky to be standing in the same room with people that were only a little wary of my future success instead of howling for my blood. The owner most likely just wanted to shake my hand and look me in the eyes. I would have wanted to do the same thing had I been in his shoes.

The drive home was a long one. The 4-hour drive to Virginia seemed to take forever. My heart was racing. I had dodged a big bullet. I thought to myself: *We all have limitations.*

You know being human, you can get hurt. You bleed when you are cut. You can break a bone when you fall. You can stop breathing when you choke. You can physically die at any moment from any number of reasons. Your soul is a different story. A soul hurt is a different kind of hurt all together.

I didn't spend my days wondering why disaster had befallen me. I knew why everything was happening. What I couldn't understand completely was how to remedy the West Palm project. In order to fix it, I needed to understand how we got into this situation in the first place. My soul was hurting because I couldn't figure out the *how*. My soul was hurting because I was the only one that could fix this. Every day, the pain in my soul seemed to get worse. The physical hurt of exhaustion was not a problem. I could work as long as I needed by this time, averaging 17 to 18 hours a day. This soul-pain was a different kind of battle all together. It would be a battle of wits and brain power. I needed to stop hurting. I had to fight three battles at a time, delegating where possible. I knew that no matter how badly I wanted a problem to go away, I had to take it head on. The damage wouldn't stop until I figured out the how.

At this point in my life, I had run out of inspiration, and no one was there to inspire me. Throughout my life, I had relied on others to create that inspiration - my mentors. They helped me get to where I was in life. Now, I had to create my own inspiration to get where I wanted to go: back in the black.

Starting with West Palm, I determined to figure out the how. I was certain I could do it. This project had started off fine in 2010, and I needed to know where it went off course. By now, I knew that the trouble was more than a bad subcontractor or the DOL. Somehow, this project had strayed. I needed to know where.

Around January 2014, after finishing another extraordinarily painful project, I called my construction operation manager, Dan. Based in Tampa, he was technically the best construction man I'd had in the southeast division of the company. With 35 years of building experience, he was one of the best builders I have ever met in the business.

Having just been through hell on the Tampa project I mentioned earlier, Dan had his hands almost free. Before I let him get slammed again, I asked him for one big favor. Point blank, I asked him if he would be willing to raise Polu Kai off the sea floor. He said, "What do you need Sean?"

"Dan, I need you to work at the West Palm Beach project on a daily basis, commuting home on the weekends until the project is complete."

Never having asked him anything like that kind of a favor before, I explained to him the pitfalls of failure. Failure here would be the end of PKS. If we did not finish the work, the bonding company and the bank would take over my business.

He said, "Are you sure you have the money to fix this?"

I said, "No, but I will think of something."

He accepted and jumped into the task. I would have been reluctant to ask anyone else to go into this hole. Before his involvement, the project was lost and lacking any direction. I knew that it needed his fresh eyes: eyes I could trust that belonged to a man who would shoot straight because he understood the work.

Nearing the end of my patience and before I could take action, I received the resignation of the current West Palm PM. It was no surprise to Dan. I figured that the PM couldn't take the pressure anymore. The writing was on the wall; I was going to have to terminate him because of the lack of progress and the failure to stop the cost promises made the previous year. He found a new job and resigned gracefully. I didn't blame him.

I held fast all of these issues. They were my responsibility. Even though I didn't have the how yet, I felt ashamed of our situation. The fire protection system we were installing was intended to protect the veterans and the families that visited that hospital. That was another reason we would not fail. I told Dan that he would have my full support.

Dan's ability to take the previous projects out of the fire in the recent past was enough proof for me to believe he had the courage and intellect to accomplish this feat as well. With my knowledge of contracting, along with his expert knowledge of construction and ability to work with all parties directly, we would create an opportunity for success. I would listen to Dan's unadulterated assessment, and then I would go to town.

Dan had a month to figure out what was going on down in West Palm. We set up a conference call between Dan, Dawn, and me. The news was doom and gloom. I always believed that Dan had his own lightning storm following him. I mean that in the most affectionate way.

When we would meet on other issues, I would laugh because he provided the worst of the worst-case scenarios. He would have been a good Marine. He told me exactly how it was. Over time, he earned my trust. I believed that he was a good advisor. Lucky for me, his predictions never came true, because he was excellent at warning us of potential problems so we could address them from the start.

His estimate to complete West Palm soared above $2 million. This figure was up from the $800,000 that I mentioned earlier. We had already paid the new sub over $1 million. I didn't have another $1 million lying around to pay that amount. After all, I was on a time and materials contract with the new sub because no one else would clean up the mess for a fixed price. Believe me, I had asked. I told Dan that I would be down soon. Then I cleared my mind of the clutter and set to work.

When you have a situation like this, when you are relying on others to give you the best and worst possible outcomes, many thoughts rush through your mind. To stay focused, you have to dismiss them. You have to go back to the beginning of the problem. Like a good detective, you have to look at every piece of data. So I began at the beginning.

The beginning of the West Palm project started with an original estimate generated in my Tampa office under the direction of Oscar and his loyal estimator, the one who vouched for him on the bid issue. Though I conducted the final negotiations and provided the caveats, I relied on them for my job quote info. At the time, everything seemed to be in order. PKS won the West Palm contract in September 2010.

Under great pressure to make the award, we held the negotiation with lots of caveats before September 30th, the end of the federal fiscal year. It was not an uncommon thing to make awards just before the federal fiscal year end. It happened every year. The funding would be lost if the money towards the project wasn't obligated.

The problems began shortly after that in early 2011, when the chosen electrical subcontractor, the husband of a now ex-employee, beat out two other high-caliber sub vendors. The margins were close. He had worked with us before, and I really didn't mind as long as everyone was playing fair. I only found out that he was involved after the contract was negotiated and won. I was assured that the bid process had integrity and that, as Oscar put it, we need to do the right thing and award to the spouse of the employee. After all, he was qualified and had the low bid.

Coincidentally, this employee was not the lead estimator, but she worked under the chief estimator at the time. I did worry and express my concerns, and I was reassured that we would be fine. I didn't have the facts or suspicions of Oscar's extracurricular business activities at that time. I trusted him. If I didn't, I would have delved into the bid deeper. Why would I set myself up to fail? He was on the bond. Why would he set himself up to fail as well?

The next red flag is one that I actually caught: the sub starting work without a bond. I have a standing rule in my company. Any construction subcontract over $250,000 requires a payment and performance bond. No ands ifs or buts, and no one can amend that policy but me. Only in the rarest cases I

I allow an exception, and security is still provided in some form.

Yet this guy was working without any security. I came down hard on everyone at the time and stopped him from working. I threatened to remove him from the job if no bond was produced. Since his contract was over a million, you can understand why I would do that.

Promises were made, and after a bit of a struggle on his part, he presented a payment and performance bond, along with a letter from the bonding company telling us that payments would be made to them, as our sub would be under funds control.

At the time, I had never really researched funds control, but I understood it now because I was going through it. It was another red flag. Funds control was more a negative than a positive, though it was necessary sometimes. To me, I thought it added security because money from the job would not be disbursed by him; the bonding company would protect their behind, thus protecting me. So I allowed the sub to continue.

The other part of the how started in Oct 2011, when the DOL showed up and launched the investigation on the sub (the employee's husband). I notified his bonding company in late 2011, per the bond requirements. I still felt safe that I could control this situation. Then it happened. By the end of 2011, the government, which had already paid us almost 80% of the job, rejected pretty much all of the work performed by my sub. I directed my sub to fix this problem, threatening action against his bonding company. These were the facts as I saw them so far.

By the spring of 2012, PKS had the DOL ruling, and the sub's bonding company declared bankruptcy. And then the sub walked off the job, never to come back, and filed for bankruptcy protection.

PKS implemented the plan to complete work with a backup sub (I'll call them NSC). In October 2012, we settled with the DOL for the first time. PKS issued checks to the individuals listed in the DOL complaint by the beginning of December of 2012. We really thought that we were going to make it after that.

Yet, here we were in 2013, with the work still not complete and with projected costs rising more than $2 million over the original total contract to my firm. No one could explain why we were going to spend $5.7 million to complete a $3.2 million award. The government had us dead to rights. In reality, they should have fired us. It was a mess. And in my careful investigation to understand the how, I was missing something critical.

The next three steps I took turned the tide of this ongoing struggle.

Step One: I was going to get to the project. Now that I was briefed, I went back and read the entire contract again: negotiation correspondences, the scope of work, and our original proposal. Since I was involved in that agreement the first go around way back in 2010, I read it again. I also read every pertinent email exchanged between us and the client regarding the project. This review would be key later on. I completed the project paper and electronic review before I reached the project.

And because another set of eyes never hurt, I also had with me my trusted secret weapon, Dawn. (I am sure when she reads the book she will appreciate that description. If you know her like I do, you will know that she is very modest about what she does at her job.) The first thing I did when I met Dan at the project trailer was the simplest task of the day. I asked for the project documents they were working with. I reviewed them and matched them to what I knew to be the contract.

My heart immediately sank when Dan described his view of the contract. He showed me the spec book and the site drawings. With one glance, I knew immediately why we were in trouble. The project he handed me covered four buildings' worth of work, not the main building that we had originally negotiated.

After some debate, I showed Dan what we had agreed upon with the client originally, before the contract was awarded. This agreement was what the old PM had used, I assumed. Up until that point, Dan had not seen the files I showed him.

The project had to be de-scoped (reduced work) prior to the award of the contract. How the spec book he had on the table got there was a mystery to me. I had my suspicions, but it was too late. We had already done way more work than we agreed to do.

On top of that, the extra work done by the old sub was wrong and was now being redone by NSC. We were providing a Cadillac fire alarm system at our own expense. Change orders had previously been requested on the project, but they were rejected. I now understood why. The negotiation and the originally scoped work were not included in those requests; so the government reps working the job, who had been replaced several times, would not know that they were in fact change orders. It wasn't a lot of money compared to the losses we were taking, but we should be paid on what we'd done. From what I saw on-site, I knew I could fix some of the problem.

Dan understood the work, and he walked me through the whole project. Some of his cost projections relied on government direction to do work that was not in our original scope. He smiled and said, "I will work up the cost pricing and send it to you."

I could have died that day. *Sean, why didn't you get here sooner?* I berated myself. I knew the answer: I was rocked by so many waves at the same time that I had to rely on others to handle some of them.

Dawn looked at me and said, perplexed by my reaction to the revelations, "Are you are going to make it?" And then she added with trepidation, "Are we going to make it?"

I said to Dawn, "I can fix this; it's just going to take some time and resources. I now know *how* we got into this mess."

Knowing the how took a huge weight off my mind and eased some of that soul hurt. My investigation had been worthwhile.

I had dinner with Dawn and Dan that night. I took them to a quiet restaurant on the water. As we talked, I discussed with them a specific plan to fix this project. I told Dan that I appreciated his service but that I was going to push him to his limits. I also told him that I believed in him and would stand by his side through this ordeal.

Step 2: I called NSC and set a meeting with their principals. Before the call, I asked Dawn to audit every certified payroll they had submitted. I reviewed their contract agreement with PKS. I had my trusted attorney, John, go through the agreement again as well, just to see if I had any leverage.

Armed with the information and the review Dawn and John provided me, I set the meeting. The first thing I had to do was to point out where the agreement stipulated that NSC would stop work and amend the agreement if the contract ceiling of $400,000 had been hit. They never had. I told their vice president that their failure was a major issue, because we relied upon NSC's expert opinion as to what completing the whole contract would take.

The project manager for NSC thought that he was there to fix the rework and nothing else, he told me. The reality was that everyone could read the writing in the agreement. *Unbelievable!* I thought.

Undeterred, I told NSC that they owed us credits of nearly $140,000 in overpayment discrepancies between their certified payroll and the invoices.

You could see the blood leaving the VP's body as I described what his responsibilities were to me. I stopped short and said, "Listen, review the information I've provided, and let's form a strategy to get through this. You're in the boat with me now, and we need to finish."

The truth was that there was no ill intent with this firm. In fact, they were a family-owned business, just a lot bigger than me. NSC worried about their reputation as much as I did about mine. I needed to know if they would finish with me before I could move to step three. I reminded them that they were the only ones making a profit here and that my bond still stood on the job.

"I have a slight problem," I told them. "I don't have the extra million on hand to pay you." I had the money to pay them on their original estimate. I had not missed an invoice to date. In fact, I was overpaying them along the way.

The VP replied in his strong southern accent, "What do you propose to do, Sean? How are you going to pay us?"

I replied, "I will pay you $100,000 a month until you are paid in full. I will also personally guarantee your payments in writing. On top of that, you have my bond to pursue, should I fail. We have back logged work. I just don't have the money in hand right now."

I was not sure, but I thought that over the phone I heard Dawn fall out of her chair. She knew how bad things were, and she knew that my credit line of a million was maxed. Dan, listening to the call, actually choked. My team was stunned that I would commit all I had without knowing the end of the project.

After some time, the VP said, "I will agree to that. Do I have your word?"
I answered, "You do!"

I think NSC may have felt a little responsible here. I knew that my agreement had some merit to sue them if they should walk off. Thanks to the good Lord, they didn't. There would have been nothing left of me or Polu Kai to sue. I asked for a revised ceiling and commitment and instructed my team to proceed. I would find the $100,000 a month to pay NSC. *I always pay all of my debts,* I told myself.

Step Three: I called a meeting with the government. Dan, after much hard work, was able to give me the additional costs associated with what I considered change order work that lay outside the originally negotiated contract.

He also provided me the spec references and construction details as to why the government was wrong to direct us to do the work.

Pulling in my legal counsel, I laid out a complete argument, backed by the negotiated contract documents originally agreed. I provided a strong argument to the overstated, non-scoped documents on site. The government meeting would be a Hail Mary pass in the fourth quarter, but I had to try. Here's another *Sean life lesson: If you are going to dispute the government, make sure you have the facts on your side.*

As a courtesy, I contacted the original government negotiator via phone to let him know what I was doing. He would ultimately be called in because he was part of the contract award process. Any professional relationship we had would not survive this relationship, once I fired my shots.

The meeting was held in Tampa. I requested a face to face with the government field contracting officer in my Tampa office. He obliged. Until this point, I had never met the field contracting officer. Any apprehension or concern I felt about how he may react had to be swept aside. I had to stick to the facts and pray that he saw things my way.

We met in my conference room in Tampa. He brought his technical point of contact (POC) with him. I brought Dan and Dawn with me. Without getting technical or demanding, I humbly asked for consideration from him. Point by point, I explained my company's position. We were being directed to do work that was not negotiated. I had with me the supporting documentation, and I showed him where we felt the ship went off course. The complete specs that the government provided described a completely different project then what was negotiated.

I explained that I would be forced to file a claim against the government, because the facts demonstrated a great injustice had been done to my firm. I further stated that the drawings provided were for a different type of fire alarm system all together and that they were not applicable, except for maybe a guide. I added that I understood I had a duty to proceed under federal law and that I was fully aware of my responsibilities. Finally, I asked for a second chance to provide these details, in an effort to overturn the previous no decisions rendered prior to this meeting.

Intently listening to me throughout my presentation of the facts, he said very little. His response was confident and concise. "I pride myself as a contracting officer to do my job in the best interests of the government. I am proud to say that I have never had a claim on a project like yours until today. I really would like to work with you. I will grant you the opportunity to convince me that the government owes you additional money. If that is the case, then I will make the responsible ruling and deal with the legal officials. Just the same, if I don't feel the government owes you money, I will let you know. It is up to you, after that."

"Sir," I replied, "all I want is a chance to put the information in front of you so that you can see what I see."

"Agreed!" he said. "Get it to me."

Even though I could have attacked the government for a multitude of failures on their end, I thanked the contracting officer for not firing me and told him directly that I would not fail. "I will complete this project or die trying. I am a US Marine. You have to kill us to stop us from completing a mission."

He cracked a smile, "The emphasis is not necessary. You have a good reputation, Sean. You have gone through hell with your subs and the DOL. We know that. Send the data over, and I will let you know what we think."

They left the office, and you could feel the excitement in the air. The amount of money we requested was the $380,000 we had already spent to do the extra work. Not only that, there was a current contract direction that could cost upwards of $300,000 that was not part of the original scope. The officer would review our arguments and provide direction. I had raised my keel and fitted new timbers. My ship was rising from the deep.

Here's the catch. I know you may think that dealing with West Palm was the only thing I was doing. The truth is, we lost $3 million in one year! Believe it or not, sinking is the easiest part. Getting back to sea level and rebuilding, if you're able, is the hardest part. So I not only engaged every project, I engaged every employee to gather every resource for rebuilding.

First I held a meeting with my executive staff. I explained that I would be cutting my pay by 40%. I told them I would cut my pay until we recovered enough to unfreeze salaries. They all on their own initiative joined in taking pay cuts. They were going to stick it out. I capped the limits of their cuts to 15%. I and my wife, who worked for the firm in HR, would take the brunt. No one would know, and I didn't tell the employees, at least not right away.

Then I met privately with my southeast division and my mid-Atlantic employees in early 2013. I delivered the message in person and then I answered questions. I explained to them how bad a shape we were in. I advised them that if they wanted to jump ship, now was the time to do so. I advised them that we had a plan, but if they chose to leave, they may be saving someone else's job. I was going to have to freeze salaries. People in the company knew we were in trouble, but they had no idea how much.

When I met the staff, I told them how much I cared about them and that I was sorry this was happening. I didn't want to lose any of them, even if there were a few that drove me nuts. They knew that they were number one and that I put my family crew first.

Polu Kai believed in top pay and benefits. We provided company vehicles to all of our superintendents and VPs. We never failed to provide good company bonuses every year.

So you could have heard a pin drop when I told them of the salary freeze. When I said that I didn't have enough information to provide a firm date on recovery, the morale fell instantly. "I have a plan." That's all I could say. I would follow my plan and offer severance packages that varied depending on years in service.

This talk was very hard on me. Some of these employees were very close to me. I had employees that went back to the hurricane days. Their employee ID numbers were in the single digits. I did not share the $3 million loss number, which was not final at the time. I relayed to them that we were going to take a major hit. Our projects were in trouble.

My annual payroll at the end of 2012 still exceeded $5 million. Including the fringe benefits and overhead, it neared $7 million a year. Our employee costs were way out of whack, even though we dropped from 110 to 73 personnel by January 2013. Around the time I was speaking to them, more cuts had to happen. The projects just weren't there to support the personnel I had on the books. Justifying our need for downsizing was not necessary, and most knew it. We had personnel on top of each other supporting personnel who were supporting personnel.

Some employees went quietly during this process. There was no job for them; so they left. Others acted out and challenged me, openly blaming me for everything. They let me know that the downturn wasn't fair to them. One even told my management team that he was going to sue me. Whatever the case, wrongful termination did not apply here. What's the government going to say, "You have to pay someone to work for you," when you have lost millions? There was no choice in the matter; these were financial decisions, not retributive layoffs.

Unfazed, I prepared to do what was necessary, even if people in the ranks bad mouthed me. They had already been rated by the executive team, who also identified troublemakers. They were already being closely managed. I had already planned on taking care of a few of them personally, with or without the current situation.

I promised my team that I would keep everyone updated. "Good, bad, or indifferent, I will talk to you if you call me with a question." I felt that I was a good communicator, but I'd been overwhelmed by circumstances lately. I told them that we would come out of this slump. To call it a catastrophe would be an understatement and would send the wrong message. I called the meeting to control the message and keep people engaged and focused. Interestingly, the ones who shouted the loudest about how we would come back were the ones that ended up out the door first. The true professionals went back to work. They knew what needed to be done. They would stick around. Besides, in their minds they knew they could get another job if they needed one.

You can judge a company by the accountants keeping the books. If you see a good accountant leave an organization during tough times, something bad is probably about to happen there. Well, in my case, none of my accounting staff left the building. I was glad, not only for the good omen but also because I would need my accountants for the path forward. I was about to take my next step. They were about to get their degrees in the school of hard knocks.

By mid-spring 2013, we were finishing some of the medium-to-worse contracts. Every day, I challenged my team to complete their work. I assigned my lawyer the task of taking on eight major legal actions. Up until this point, I despised the legal actions because I had learned from my battles early on in my company's growth that everyone loses in legal battles. This time I felt I had no choice. I had to fight. I had two lawsuits to defend that came at me from private entities related to the West Palm defaulted sub.

In reality, they were claims that would turn into lawsuits if settlement couldn't be reached. My lawyer also worked with one of the top DOL lawyers in the country to defend us from the previously settled wage dispute with DOL.

The DOL case was a serious threat to our recovery. Their decision to ask us for more money, after we settled in December of 2012, was a real setback. We appealed the decision in 2013. Now we had to wait for the answer from the DOL before we could assess the new threat hanging over our heads. The client was already holding all the money we were due on West Palm by direction of the DOL. If I'd learned anything from my friends who had previous encounters with them, it was that little guys hardly ever beat them. They had extraordinary powers and protections under the law.

I fired off lawsuits against the default West Palm subcontractor, seeking bankruptcy protection against any assets they may show as a business. I filed a legal claim on any assets his bankrupt bonding company had with the trustee from the commonwealth of PA. All these suits were long shots, but I had to try. You never knew. I also fired off a personal guarantee lawsuit against the owner of the now-defunct West Palm subcontractor.

I fought back throughout 2013. To me, this fight was just the beginning of the voyage, not the end. Everyone in my way, especially those that aimed to hurt my family, would all get to know me a little better. Some would grow to like me, even to respect me. Others would despise me. Either way, I was implementing my plan. I had already taken control of the battlefield. They just didn't know it yet. Besides, I had just the general counsel and team of accountants to do what was necessary. My counsel was just the advocate I needed. And Dawn was just the administrator I needed. She ran her department like shock troops. They were my administrative special forces.

It goes without saying that when you commit yourself to legal action, you're going to spend money that you may not recoup. Whether you're going after the government or a private company, you need to have your ducks in a row. Even if you are found to be right, you don't necessarily win. There may be no pot of gold. You have to decide if the end result is going to pay off. Sometimes you get a judgment, but there is no compensation to give because it is already gone on legal fees and court costs. Legal action can be a high-stakes distraction if you get buried in paperwork, like we were.

John asked for everything. There was a flood tide of information, and my crew took most of 2012 and 2013 to provide it to him. The accounting team started the effort in late 2012, delivering everything they had - at least, what was in their control.

Much of the information needed to win these battles came from reviewing months of field project paperwork, which was a tedious process. Since my lawyer was taking my claims on contingency, he absorbed part of the risk, too. I felt strongly that we would win by completing the projects and thereby eliminating any failure to complete defense my opponents might have. As soon as was feasible, we would start the claims process, armed with the actual costs associated with the loss. We prepared reams of supporting documents in binders and disks. Only an attention-to-detail type would get through it, and I had some of that type on my crew. My accounting and administration groups were doing a stellar job.

In the spring of 2013, the bank representatives came knocking on my door for the June renewal. Each year, we went through an underwriting evaluation and assessment. Usually it involved the audited year-end financial statement, a copy of our work-in-progress schedule, and a personal financial statement. With all of my major resources tied to the company, my personal financial statement was now a negative one million dollars. I had nothing, and they knew it.

The bank representative who normally worked with me was gone. Instead, I was met with a serious fellow. His title simply read: "Vice President, Asset Resolution Team." He was with the asset recovery division of the bank: I'll call him Bob. The asset recovery division consisted of experts sent to distressed debtors to determine whether they can pay their debts.

If you ever find yourself in a meeting with a guy who can effectively shut down your business, do the following. Step one: smile. Step two: have your plan ready. Step three: make sure you have already completed steps in the plan and made progress so that you can show the positive impact of said plan.

I did all those things. The gentleman sized me up carefully. I already knew he was sent to me to decide if I could ever pay the money I owed the bank. During the meeting, we reviewed my financials, my back log, and my plan to eliminate the ongoing threats to my firm. Everything he was reading in our 2012 financial statement had come to pass. Now we had our first quarter data from 2013.

The news wasn't outstanding, but it was positive. Sales were brisk, and we were showing a profit on the new work. Construction business revenue always slows during the holidays. Working during that time of year is a bit challenging considering the frozen ground and frequent rains and snows.

Spring usually brings the dollars flowing when work can actually proceed.

The other thing I had going during the meeting was a surprise. In October 2011, my firm was selected for a major contract with the Veterans Administration in the southeast. It was a 5-year, multiple award contract with funding capacity not to exceed $100,000,000. The selection process had taken almost a year and half. We won that major contract. And we were beginning to win other competitive contracts, just like I had envisioned.

Normally, I might have patted myself on the back. We presented these successes as business as usual. We relied on our positive growth and track record over the last 5 years. Now, the fruits of those labors were paying off.

To demonstrate our viability as a firm, I pointed out to the asset recovery VP that we were not retreating from our responsibilities. Rather, we had been swallowed by a perfect storm of recent events. I explained to him that I knew he was there to call my line of one million dollars. I also let him know that if he did so, he would have almost a zero chance of collecting, because the bonding company was first in line. He probably didn't like that point, but he got it. He was an old pro.

We made promises to make some small, achievable progress payments before the end of the year. I figured that the bank would step in at any moment to get what it could, but a million-dollar loss for them was not something they wanted to have on their bottom line, either. The bank put me on a very short leash. They required monthly internal financial statements, along with a plethora of other controls.

They were no different than the bonding company, who had more to lose. Fortunately, they were still backing me, and that good faith went a long way for the bank. If the elephant in the room (the surety) was willing to add more risk to my company, he couldn't have a better explanation for his superiors. I asked the bank to trust me. We could overcome the past; we just needed time. They did not default the line, thank God.

Now I could regroup. I could rebuild my boat and prepare to seize the changing tide.

Chapter 16:

Clearing the Sky

Sean P. Jensen

THE downsizing of my organization moved quickly. Though natural attrition or resignations, we cut our payroll costs by nearly a million dollars, and the relief showed. Having moved from a negative $2 million to a negative $1 million, we were closing the gap to breaking even, at least on paper. With the salary freeze implemented at the end of 2012 and cuts to executive pay, including 40% of my compensation, PKS was now able to redirect that money towards the debt we'd incurred. We sold unused equipment and turned it into cash. I took the $550,000 personal income tax return from the losses and put that directly back into the company. As painful as that move was, it showed the commitment the outside supporters wanted to see. Closing out the little battles cleared the way to success on the larger battles.

Now focused, I worked to complete larger objectives. It was possible to spend just as much time and effort trying to recoup $25,000 as you would trying to recoup $250,000. My time was precious, and so was my lawyer's. I took small hits all around the company. But the time and effort I recouped for me and my team was priceless.

We made our payments, as I promised NSC, and we started working on legitimate change orders that could help recoup lost money from the project during the crisis. We were definitely asked to perform things outside of our contract. The bank and bonding company were still supporting me, and for the moment a thread of light shone through the clouds.

It was time to talk to my crew. Before the end of September 2013, I updated my employees again. By now, they had seen the mass exodus of personnel, some good and some bad. I didn't have time to explain all of my decisions. Most times, I just acted. I was running on muscle memory of past experiences. I had no time to share my vision. The stakes were very high. I had noticed that morale was low and attitudes were crashing. I had to act again. The excerpts from that meeting are below. They are very telling of my frustration at the time.

Addressing the entire company from administrator to executive, I opened with short stories about my background, my childhood, and the personal struggles I'd endured. I wanted people to connect with me on a personal level. I had to grab their attention. They could pick their own personal difficulty and remember how they overcame that. I wanted them emotionally involved in what was happening then. Telling them of my early challenges and how I overcame that part of my life got their attention. And then I got to the meat and potatoes of the conversation.

"When you grow as fast as PKS has, setbacks are inevitable. Every company has trials and tribulations. We definitely have had ours. Together, today, here and now, we are going to finish turning those pages of our history, forget the setbacks, and determine to overcome the obstacles ahead. We have learned from the past mistakes and made corrections. Before we are done this year, PKS is going to get back to basics.

"I consider you all friends and part of my family. But I want you to know that I have not been pleased with some of things I have witnessed over the past year and a half. I hope I will not have to address this issue again after today, but I want you to know where I stand. So I am going to discuss it with you now.

"When you go through what we have, the stress exposes the best and worst of people. As an organization, PKS has been changed by major, devastating events. Some were our own doing, and some were beyond our control. Some were simple mistakes. Some were connected to bad management and poor oversight. Some were tied directly to crooked people that covered up their theft and fraud. Those people somehow found a way inside our organization, even though we had many controls in place.

"In the end, I have taken full responsibility for all of those factors, and I am the one who will be held accountable. I did not react to everything I saw or heard. I did in some cases. Other times, I knew that a person was leaving, and I chose to help him out the door. Still other times, I had the person's leaders talk to him. Sometimes I've spoken to you directly. In the end, I'm fighting too hard to deal with some of the disruptions and attitudes I have witnessed.

"Here are just few examples. During the crisis, people have flat-out lied to me on simple questions. I have witnessed people blaming others for their own mistakes and failure to understand a situation. Sometimes they pointed at me and said, 'It's your fault, Sean.' I don't mind taking the blame. I have walked into meetings with government officials who told me, 'We plan to terminate you for lack of performance,' when just before that I was told, 'Everything is fine. Don't worry, Sean.'

"I have seen so many things this past year. Over half the incidents have floored me. You could have knocked me over with a feather. I've seen superiors sticking up for someone who I knew was trying to hurt this company. I expect managers to open their eyes and look at all the facts. I have seen some really selfish individual behavior, and I am mystified where it has come from. I know it's not the example I have set.

"I personally believe that every one of you possesses the knowledge, skills, and abilities to be here in your positions. Many of you have grown and excelled beyond my expectations. To you I say, 'Well done and bravo! I am really proud of you.'

"It is my job to give everyone a chance at success and either correct that individual or move him along. We have worked too hard and our recovery is too important to our future to let any one employee ruin it.

"I once heard a powerful statement in a sermon. *'Your attitude is an inward feeling expressed by outward behavior. It can be seen by all without saying a word.'* Stop and think about that statement. Look at your attitude.

"While no one wants to beat a dead horse, we need to talk about the past and some of the negatives today. This meeting is not meant to be a pep talk. Before you can fully appreciate the end of my PKS update, I need you to walk with me through the last 18 months. Winston Churchill said that 'those who do not learn from history are fated to repeat it.'"

Point blank, I walked them through the losses. I talked about the banks and the bonding companies and the personal commitments I'd made. I even told them how we absorbed healthcare insurance increases, not passing on the cost to them that year. It was the right thing to do, because they had no raises. Any extra cost to them would add insult to injury. Times were tough enough.

I challenged them to improve and commit to success and promised them the following: "I will always be transparent. I have always had an open door and phone policy, and I will continue it. When you have a question or concern, talk to me about it. I will shoot you straight. You may not always like the answer you get, but it will be an honest one.

"We will provide training where it is needed; just let us know if there is a system or process where you need further clarification. I want you to have the tools and education to succeed."

Finally, I told them my expectations for the final quarter. I made them achievable. Then I left them with a promise to give everyone an extra week of vacation if our year-end financial goals were met.

That meeting was a somber occasion. We were waist-deep in battles. Still, this situation was better than being neck-deep like I was at the start of 2013. My conversation was candid and direct. But I never told them about my biggest nightmare. There were periods of time when I would wake up at night imagining that no one showed up for work.

Even the best, most competent players have fears. It's ingrained in our psyche. Naturally for an abandoned boy, mine consisted of my Polu Kai ohana leaving me.

Nightmares aside, I never lost confidence. We needed a win, something that would change the atmosphere and bring us back to basics. That win was just around the corner. The big bounce was the income tax return that I put back into the company against the debt. Along with the savings applied to the larger projects, we picked up positive gains where we projected larger losses.

The negative $1 million was still the biggest challenge. Making payments on the $1 million line of credit hanging over my head when I needed every dollar just to keep the ship afloat was very difficult. That balance had to be paid down to keep the bank interested in supporting our recovery. We were stable and rebuilding, but we weren't seaworthy yet. The continuing losses we absorbed from uncompleted projects were taking a toll on every dollar we made.

We needed a big bounce to complete rebuilding. We needed a big profit, something that could tear into our debt like the blue-roof contracts that started and restarted my company years ago. With the government shutdown looming and sequestration in full swing, we needed some good news.

An unlikely contract cleared the sky for me. Believe it or not, I had time to sell new work. Throughout the year, I continued to do just that: sell. You may have heard that work solves problems. There is a lot of truth to that saying.

We had already started on one particular project earlier in the year. Having had the contract for the last five years, we were always making some modest profit on the tasks. When I got the news that there was a serious project on the horizon, I got excited.

One problem was that the contract was getting ready to expire. If not extended, our firm would lose the new opportunity. I was bummed, because any profit was good profit, and this was not the time to lose more people or work. I turned up the sales heat with justification after justification to convince them to extend. You can imagine I was a real charmer.

Then out of the blue, just as I thought it was lost, the client extended our contract. Not just that, they also added project scope, exponentially growing the project to double the previous four years of work on the entire contract! There was so much work to be done that the client wondered if we could do it all.

They had an emergency requirement. They needed us to gut a medical building, completely removing all of the environmental hazards. My language was being spoken to me. It was like listening to Hawaiian for the first time; it was beautiful. It was a major task, unlike anything we had done to date for them. The demolition and abatement requirements were extensive.

Suffice it to say, I was going to seize the opportunity. Though the client's identity will remain confidential, they were in a real pickle. They'd made promises to another government agency that they would remediate all environmental issues in this building by a now almost impossible date.

I was their only solution, because we had a contract in place that covered their exact needs. The work was something that 4 people normally handled for me. Now, we would need 200 people to remediate an entire building full of asbestos and other hazardous materials by December 2013. *Wow!* I thought to myself. *This might be the Hail Mary I needed.*

To me, this extension was like the blue-roof contracts. Big contracts like these brought in bigger profits. Yes, I had just downsized the company and had no money to pay 200 people, but what the hell.

You've got to grab at the golden ring when it goes by, right?

After some convincing, the client and I negotiated the work. I explained that I understood the performance rules of the contract and that I would meet the 51% cost of labor performance without violating any federal rules. I also explained that the contract had the prompt payment clause in the contract: 14 days for construction; 30 days for service contracts on all client-approved invoices.

I asked them for prompt approval and timely processing, given the magnitude of the project. They had a history of late approvals, which extended my invoice payments to over 60 days in past cases. The good thing was that they always paid.

I also knew that if I could get past the first invoice, we could make the arrangement work, because we would get into a work billing cycle receiving progress payments during the project.

They agreed, extended my contract, and asked me for a firm, fixed price: a lump sum to complete the job. I priced the project, including regular labor, overtime labor, disposal, and the bells and whistles I'd need to perform the work on time to meet their impossible date.

After a short review of my proposal and some back and forth negotiations, they accepted pending the received funds from the agency. Then we could go to work. This extension would be mean substantial profits for my firm if we finished on time or early. However, the client knew they were asking me the impossible if there were any delays to the project start. I had been working for them for almost 5 years, and I had never seen anything like it. I knew that if we didn't meet the deadline, I could put a fork in my future. I was doing a quadruple doubling down against the house, who for the most part almost always wins.

The client called and said, "Go!" I quickly hired the people I needed and began the project. Then just like that, the unthinkable happened. On September 30, 2013, the government shut down. Much to my dismay, so did most of my projects. With no government supervision, work stopped. The few remaining critical projects, like the home run project, were allowed to continue.

While there was much banter between Capitol Hill and the president, politics once again had thrown a curve ball at my company. I had some cash on hand, but not enough to go over a month. How would I make payroll? How would I handle this indefinite closure?

Now I wondered if this contract would even work. I had no back-up plan. I owed millions of dollars to vendors and creditors. There was no one working in the government to hit the pay button on all of the outstanding invoices sent by my firm. My world had crashed again!

I wondered: *What else can go wrong?* Cash was so tight. And with all the guarantees I made, I did not have enough money to make payroll the final week of the 15-day shutdown. I didn't even know if the government would reopen. They owed us millions of dollars on outstanding invoices; some were two months old because there was no one to push the buttons.

I was freaking out. If we didn't get paid or if the government shut down lasted longer than a month, I would have to lay everyone off. I knew we were owed the money, but when would it come? I couldn't ask people to come to work without pay. Legally, I had to pay them, and there could be consequences if I didn't. Hell! I was already knee-deep dealing with what should have been someone else's trouble with the DOL, and I certainly didn't want any more trouble.

I knew some employees would come to work. But I had already put everyone through enough. I convinced my wife to make payroll, borrowing against our retirement money, the last of any reserve we had. That was another sad day in the Great Recession tragedy, one that I will not soon forget. Thankfully, the government reopened, and I paid back the borrowed money. I did not say a word to my staff about borrowing from myself. Only the most senior people knew. I was worried about perception. It wouldn't take much to get people to jump off the ship now. I'd survived another desperate moment in what would be the longest roller coaster ride year of my life. The silver lining was that if we could survive this trial, we were definitely going to be seaworthy and ready to sail on a favorable tide under a clear sky.

As for that emergency project, we did make a great profit happen. Countless hours, countless people, and a few client surprises later, we finished the project shortly before Christmas. 2 months before, I'd never even known the task existed. I didn't think too hard about it; like my previous adventures, I just got it done. I had awesome support from my team and vendors, who never faltered on my relationships. I paid them every nickel they were owed, and they bore with me the pain of slower-than-usual pay. I had earned and maintained their trust by helping many of them over the last decade.

PKS still faced some tough sailing. We had not received any answer to the DOL question, nor had we resolved the change orders on the West Palm project. The legal cases were in review, and two of the decisions on our claims were pending in spring 2014. By the end of the year, we had completed all other failing projects, except West Palm. The project in Hawaii was quietly moving to completion. The danger seemed to be over.

Everyone accepted from me that litigation was certain to follow if they continued with their hard-line positions. For now, all seemed eerily quiet, I stuck to the original plan we presented the bonding company and the bank. Yes, there were some minor deviations around the large fluctuations. Clouds were passing, but the sky held more sun than shadow.

I am not certain if luck played into this at all, but that emergency project, along with some generous profitability on other projects, brought my equity up to $18,000 dollars. We were back in the black for the first time in 2 years. I had a little more than I had when I started the company in '02. When you're starting with an equity balance of negative $2 million and you're on the verge of losing everything, and then you hit $18,000 dollars, you have to give back to those who helped you. I did. I honored my agreement with my staff and gave them the extra week off. I also made sure that everyone got a bonus at Christmas time.

The salary freeze was understood, even though disappointing. I had given bonuses every year, even in years we weren't so profitable. The bank or bonding company was not going to care if the equity was $12,000 or $68,000. What would they say to me? *Worst recovery ever! You swung your entire company around in one year, recovering almost to zero equity from negative $2 million. You suck, Sean!*

Not even close; no one balked at my rewarding my team. When I explained to my bonding agent what I did, he replied, "Give me a break, Sean. Who comes back from the dead like that?"

And when he saw our financial statement, he said, "I knew you could do it. I would question anyone else's capability, but never yours." If he only knew how close to the edge we'd been, he might not have thought that way. As amazed as they had been to see our loss, they were just as amazed at our recovery. Now the big question I had to answer was: *Is this for real?*

You see, true recovery is sustained recovery, inching upward every year until your ship's sails are full. It's not short-lived windfalls. It's not chance profit.

I am a firm believer in destiny and karma. During 2013, all of the kindness and generosity I showed others in life came back to me tenfold and all at once. There were too many stories to share, and I am once again indebted to those who stood by me. *It's not over until it's over; I have a few more fish to fry,* I thought going into the New Year.

2014 started out no differently than 2013. We were still in the hole with the bank, having paid down $150,000 of our debt. We still owed $850,000. And we were still just above zero equity. We still owed buyout payments to former partners. The bonding company was not letting up, and funds control still ruled the day.

However, there were slight, noticeable differences. The morale was up! I guessed that the bonuses and the extra week off really paid dividends in happiness. My people were smiling again. I held my senior management meeting, as I did every year. This time I called in some favors and flipped the script. Instead of 3 long days in a boardroom setting, we were going on a field trip.

After reviewing the year with my team, you couldn't slap the smiles off everyone's faces. Evidently some believed that we were through the worst. We were coming out of this dark time. I was proud of them. I told them they would all make great Marines. To demonstrate that point, I wanted to show them what we jarheads were really about. Get your permission slips signed; we are all going on a field trip!

I would give my executive team a personal tour of the National Museum of the Marine Corps. I told them that if they really wanted to understand me and my personality, it was time they learned about the United States Marines. Through a mutual friend I managed to get the executive officer of Officers Candidate School to give them a commander's brief on the selection and building of US Marine officers. No offense to my enlisted brother and sisters, but good training is good training.

I capped off the day with a demonstration of the Marine Corps Martial Arts Program provided by Marines Corps premier hand-to-hand combat instructors and one of the creators of the program, Lt. Col. Joe Shusko. Three of my executives were prior service veterans: 2 Army and 1 Air Force. We ribbed each other at work all the time. All of us veterans seemed to understand each other because we knew what it meant to serve.

When it comes to the Marine Corps, we jarheads proudly admit to being a different breed. Most other military branches believe we are all crazy. Any Marine will tell you that we are mission-accomplishment oriented people who take initiative to succeed, regardless of the difficulty of any given mission.

My prior service guys had never taken the time to learn what being a Marine was truly about. Throughout the day they learned about impossible battles like Belleau Wood, The Frozen Chosin, Iwo Jima, and modern-day battles like Fallujah.

Our business struggles were not life or death, I told them. But for the Marines in those battles, their struggles were life or death. We gained inspiration from those brave men and women. My leaders learned about the inspiration from those brave men and women. My leaders learned about character, service, and sacrifice ingrained in me by my early mentors.

I was having a field day as I heard them commenting throughout the day, saying to me that they never knew what being a Marine was all about. The misunderstanding that Marines were all crazy seemed to melt away as the day went on. My prior service brethren and non-veteran leaders were all learning about what being a Marine meant to me. They were beginning to understand how and why we all carry the honor, courage, and commitment we have with us every day.

"You guys aren't half bad after all," my Air Force VP said to me. Laughing, I told him thanks. But for me to share with them the history and great teachings of moral value that had been instilled in me as a young man was a truly a fulfilling personal experience.

My favorite moment of the day occurred in the early morning. We finished the Marine movie at the front of the museum. My Cuban ambassador VP, Randy, got up after the movie ended, saying loudly to everyone around, "That explains everything, Sean!" like he'd finally figured me out after working with me for 6 years. I smiled to myself and put my arm around his shoulder. He continued, "I don't know how you got us through this last year, but I have a better idea where you found the skills to do it."

I felt as if he understood that every decision I had made along the way was not just about me. My motivation came from the Marines, my family, and my company.

Kahili Mahi

Standing Strong

Sean P. Jensen

Chapter 17:

The Fish Fry

Sean P. Jensen

WHEN it comes to legal matters with the government, there comes a time where there are no more places to hide. The legal claims process seems to take forever. When you endure months or years (in some claims) of time stalling and promised decisions by government officials, all of which delay the process for eternity, you feel like you can't wait for the day when they run out of time and the claim is taken out of your client's hands. During that waiting time, your claim and the losses you have already endured get drowned in procedures. Then your claim finally gets heard by a judge.

In my case, these claims were both over a year old. The losses had appeared on PKS's books 2 years before, because I could not file the claims until I was done with the work. Having waited for months to get the government contracting officers' negative determination on my claims, I couldn't start the appeals process.

Then you realize that your understanding of the facts is finally going to be reviewed by a non-interested, impartial third party. The people who ruled against you also understand that. Contractors will spend thousands if not hundreds of thousands of dollars of their money to get their day in court. Mounting costs to produce the claim include legal fees, time, and much of your administrative employees' time to provide all of the backup. That's on top of the losses you already incurred on the job and additional costs paid to contractors and employees added to whatever they are trying to take from you as free work. What starts out as a hundred-thousand-dollar claim can double by the time it is all said and done.

Reimbursement of legal fees is not always a guarantee if you win, either. It depends on the case and the judge. The whole ordeal of going to court for justice is a major undertaking. So you have to understand why people like me don't make a habit of going after the government. You don't file claims unless you are resolute in your case. Even then, you can still lose if you don't survive the legal process and get to an impartial judge.

The process begins simply; it starts with a disagreement. You ask for relief from the government, like a change order or more time. They respond by rejecting or accepting the request. Then you go before the contracting officer, the decision maker on the project who has control of the purse strings and has a warrant power of authority to commit government money. Only the officer can do that while you perform a contract. They are required to act like a judge, being fair and making impartial rulings.

So if the government is not acting fairly, ruling in favor of someone like myself, if necessary, the contracting officer decides disagreements between the contractor and the client representatives. They also resolve numerous other issues like contract questions or clarifications as needed.

If the contracting officer decides against you on a cost issue or scope issue, then you have the right as the contractor to ask them for a final determination. This gives the contracting officer one last chance to rule before the contractor appeals to the courts.

Polu Kai had long passed those parts, and we had received our decisions. We filed an appeal to a federal judge in both of my cases.

Once you get to federal court, you have to prove your case, costing you more money. If you survive all of that rigmarole and still don't back down, the judge will talk to the counsel for each party to see if there is an opportunity to open a settlement discussion before the trial.

When everyone knows that you're close to a trial, people on the other side really start reviewing your claim. That could be good for you or bad for you. There is really no more blame to issue and no more bluffing from contracting folks who just want you to go away. I say that in jest, because the vast majority of government contracting officers are going to do the right thing.

I had gone the first ten years of business without ever having to file a claim. PKS went out of our way to resolve our issues in the field. Sometimes I thought my client was right, sometimes wrong. In those cases, I gathered the facts and convinced them of their error. Other times, I did the work because I believed they were entitled to it.

That being said, once the lawyers take over, everyone knows that the law is going to be applied by an outside party. Things can get interesting. The whole record gets scrutinized at this stage. If the government lawyers think there is merit to your claim, you may have a chance to discuss a settlement without a judge.

Usually, government counsel will make a legal recommendation to the federal agency they are defending as to what to do next. The agency doesn't have to follow the recommendation. But no lawyer is in the business of losing cases. For many agencies, mediation is the preferred method of handling contract disputes, because they can avoid costly legal fees and avoid embarrassment by having a large judgment against them if they lose in court. They also have to look at the manpower and resources it will take to defeat you.

In my two cases, the government waited until the very last moment to open settlement discussions, stringing me along. One case was a year and a half old from the date I filed my original case. As the trial date got closer and closer, the counsel for the other side began getting frustrated. We weren't going away. I observed and participated in what appeared to be a game of high-stakes chicken.

The opposing counsel made us offers to discuss, mediate, and even settle the cases for very low amounts during the weeks leading to the trials. These offers were paltry compared to our documented and fully-accounted losses. Through several rounds of legal motions, I thought for sure that the case was going to a judge at any moment. During those rounds, the system added even more time to the clock, delaying the trial dates. We inched closer and closer. I was nervous. Who wouldn't be?

After numerous phone discussions with my counsel, I saw clearly that the government counsel in both of my cases did not want a trial. They just didn't want to give PKS the full amount of our claims. What was at stake for me was $700,000 on one claim and $575,000 on another claim, all of which was unrelated to West Palm. The dollars may sound well and good, but they weren't really. Between subcontractors that were financially injured by having to do extra work, our unpaid work, and the legal fees, we would be lucky to see half of what I'd suffered in actual costs, even if I won both claims.

In one case, we took legal depositions of the government personnel responsible for denying my claim. The counsel for the government was so absolutely appalled at what they heard from the government witnesses during depositions that the government's lawyers immediately recommended a settlement to the contracting officer.

However, ignoring the government attorneys' counsel, this contracting officer accused me of fraud instead, elevating the situation to a new level. In response, I told the counsel for the government plainly, "Now you know what I have dealt with for two years. Based on the facts and back-up I have presented the government, I welcome the Inspector General to show up at my office. He can have full access to my personnel, job file, and any information he deems important to this accusation. I have provided every payroll, every canceled check, every subcontract or purchase order, along with all correspondence related to this project. Despite my full disclosure and compliance for more than a year, this official has the audacity now to accuse me of fraud."

I paused for a moment. I needed to remain calm but insistent. I breathed deeply through my nostrils, slowly, before continuing.

"I have now hit the limit of my willingness to negotiate a settlement. I am looking forward to going to trial. I will bring a lawsuit against this agency and a personal lawsuit against this individual for slander regarding these unsubstantiated claims."

I thought to myself: *I will distribute a press release like no one has ever seen. I will call this person on the carpet publicly, because I have nothing to hide. I will not stand here and be accused falsely when we have been honest and forthright throughout this arduous process.*

Recognizing my frustration and obviously harboring his own frustrations with the stubborn contracting officer, the government counsel said quietly, "Sean, we wouldn't be here if we believed those accusations." Picking up my lawyer's jaw from the floor after he heard my sudden, passionate rebuttal, I left.

The attorney from the government had phone calls to make, and we had other fish to fry. The chain of command was soon informed of the incident, and they got involved. The fraud accuser was replaced. That was the first time I ever witnessed that kind of drastic action in doing business with the government. In the end, we settled with the agency, and everyone released everyone else from future action.

In the other claim, the government and my counsel agreed to a settlement just before trial. I thought the government was bluffing their way through the case. On the other hand, our argument had strong points and weak points. My counsel was sure that we would win, but was the government really just bluffing or not? We weren't sure; so we settled on our strong points and gave up the claim on the weak points. Doubt on both sides on how the law would be interpreted drove both sides to settle. We both acquiesced to a lower figure than either of us wanted.

All in all, you don't get a headline saying that you beat the government. You get paid, and you release the government from further claims. We ended up with a little less than half of our claim amount, after we paid all parties. Even so, I was happy because we were proven right on our claims and vindicated of the false accusations of the hostile US government official. In my opinion, the two contracting officials on the government side should have been fired or retrained. I wondered to myself if we really won at all, because in our world it was a good possibility that we would see them again.

You never really know why the government decides the things they do or why people are the way they are. I believe that the power they held over us during our performance review went to their heads. I had heard stories about contractors getting screwed by both of these people before.

But these people weren't the whole government, just some barnacles hanging onto it. Many government workers represent the nation well. Our civil servants have a thankless job. Most are devoted people who give decades of service to the government. They are the backbone of our country's government. Politicians will come and go. These men and women always have to deal with the aftermath when they are gone. Having worked side by side with many in the Marines, I have a deep appreciation for their service.

Two fish were now fried. There was one to go. Resolving those two matters really helped me become more focused for my next challenge. The DOL was not going to go away quietly in the night. After waiting a year for them to deny my appeal of their reneged settlement agreement with me, I was at a cross roads. I was on the verge of completing the West Palm project, the one for which the DOL was continuing to hold hundreds of thousands of dollars in payments to which I was entitled.

I gathered my legal team once again. The prognosis wasn't good. It was 2014, three years after the DOL first entered the mix. They had wreaked havoc on this project, and their destruction had to end. In my mind, we could have ended this a long time ago if my sub's bonding company had been around. They weren't, and it was up to me to get this problem fixed.

The situation I faced basically rested with a demand that I pay another $278,000 to my subcontractor's ex-employees. Many of these people had already received payment from me the prior year. I paid them exactly what the government had directed. The only holdout finally cashed our check in the beginning of 2014, over a year after we cut it.

My options were to pay them exactly what the DOL demanded, losing another $278,000, or I could appeal to a DOL board in D.C. I knew that the appeal would take another year, based on my legal discussions. That was potentially another year out of my life I would never recover. Most likely, the board would deny my appeal and support the government administrator who denied my first one.

just don't get to sue them in federal court. You can appeal to the circuit court if denied at the board, but that won't happen for a long time. It takes forever.

I needed a third option. In my case, I had a directors and officers insurance policy, commonly called a D&O policy. Unfortunately, my policy was written in a weird way, allowing the insurance company to defend Polu Kai, not settle matters. They had already agreed to that clause in the policy. But the policy also said that I had to be the one that committed the wrong. In this case, I didn't underpay the guys. The subcontractor did, and he was now bankrupt. Still, somehow the claim now rested with me. Incredibly, I was the responsible party for breaking a law I never broke.

How the hell does that happen?

It was not like I was going to jail or something here. If I paid what the DOL demanded, then I would be in compliance with the law, which would mean that no law was broken. Yet a terrible injustice would have been done to me, my employees, and my business. A damn shipwreck was what this was!

I sat down and brainstormed for an option 3, a new settlement without a two-year appeal. I had an insurance policy that would pay to defend me, but it would not pay my subcontractor's former employees directly. I had a case against the DOL for reneging on the settlement with me. On top of that, the West Palm project was almost done, holding much needed funds to pay off my $100,000 due monthly to NSC. Any appeals would hold the job open, because money would not be released. *Good grief!* I thought.

After a few more sleepless nights, the solution hit me. If I could convince the insurance company to pay me and release them from defending me, I could work a new deal with the DOL. If I settled the DOL dispute, I could come up with some money from the recent claim wins and maybe add that to the insurance company money. I would have to get the DOL to recalculate the damages, based on the fact that I had already gotten many signed releases from the ex-employees during the first so-called settlement. (Only 13 never signed our release.) We could deduct the money I previously paid and make every party happy without two years of appeals and expenses. The previous releases protected the DOL, because we used their settlement form. I hope you're keeping up with me; it was a little blurry.

I called my legal team together and told them my plan. At first, they both tried to take in my thoughts. Legal minds do not necessarily think like sergeants unless they've been sergeants. Neither one of my counsel had ever served.

My general counsel spoke first. He told me that my idea was a little crazy. "Too many pieces!" he complained.

My DOL counsel said, "Maybe, but I think the settlement lines are closed."

After a little more discussion, they both agreed to give my idea a try. It would take a week or so to get the parties to buy into the idea. I could tell that the DOL and my insurance company might move, because no one immediately said no. By the third week, everyone was in. The insurance company would pay half of the amount due, as long as it didn't go higher than the recent demand. The underwriters would avoid a certain doubling of their liability to defend me for two years. They had already done the math, and the defense reserve listed on my policy said they would defend me up to a million dollars. I don't think anyone understood that part until I read that document 40 times. No one wanted to go to the Supreme Court with me, especially if my insurance company was going to pay for my defense. They really liked my plan now. The settlement hinged on the exact settlement number from the DOL now.

They reopened the door. Would I have to pay $165,000 or $50,000 out of pocket? They'd originally demanded $400,000 from me. Based on the $135,000 I had already paid plus the revision due to our self-audit, that number had dropped to $278,000. Taking in the release amount of deductions I had paid my sub's ex-employees, we were down to $110,000. This was the amount on which I did not have releases for monies paid previously to the ex-employees I never had.

Here was another problem for the DOL. How could they tell a judge I owed more when I had all these releases from the actual damaged parties? I never knew the truth of the underpayment. Most of these workers were claiming to be electricians when they could barely hold a ladder.

The DOL came back with an offer of $208,000 to release me from this issue. With the insurance company chipping in, we could settle for $138,000 out of my pocket. The DOL seemed to want one more pound of flesh out of me. After all, we were beating up on their investigators pretty good. They had put me through the wringer, warning that this could be a lot worse for me during one phone conversation in front of my legal counsel and other federal officials. "Pay up or it's going to be worse for you!" is how I understood their message.

Only when this process got above them did the rhetoric and tone come down. Presumably, those field investigators were feeling the heat from above. The handling of my case was appalling. My DOL lawyer commented that in her 30 years, she had never seen the DOL behave this way. By now, the most senior personnel in the DOL were getting briefed. Everyone wanted off this bus, especially me. This plan of mine was exactly what I wanted and needed. I had to be free of this West Palm nightmare. It had to be resolved.

When telling me of the final settlement reached with all parties, my general counsel, John, offered me a fine compliment. "Brilliant! I never would have thought to do that."

I am pretty sure I responded with, "You should be paying me to advise you." Then I thanked him for his efforts, of course.

PKS had managed to fry three desperately needed fish in 2014, and we were just getting started. These recovered dollars would go straight back into the company, raising our bottom line. By June, we had reached settlements with the bankruptcy court handling the remains of my bankrupt West Palm subcontractor. We even managed to recoup monies from the dead bonding company. Those long shots paid off.

We sold our bond claim to an investment group with the permission of the commonwealth of PA trustee. His position was, "You'll get paid, but I don't know when." I settled for 8.3% of our maximum claim just so that it wouldn't be my problem anymore. The claim was accepted at the contract value of $1,355,000. Of that, PKS received $112,500.

At the same time, we completed the West Palm Beach project. Having convinced the contracting officer that we were entitled to change orders, we managed to pick up a few hundred thousand dollars against the loss. After three and half years, the project construction was over. We demobilized from the site in May of 2014. The government later issued a telling past performance review:

As previously stated, the Contractor faced the challenge of his original electrical subcontractor going out of business along with his subcontractor's bonding company. Electrical Subcontractor also had issues with DOL that were passed along to prime contractor to deal with.

These problems set the contractor way behind the completion curve along with quality problems that the original electrical subcontractor caused.

Although I am rating the contractor marginal on schedule, I must give the contractor credit for staying the course, working to completion. Another contractor would have required termination.

One line read, "The contractor faced the perfect storm." Another line said, *"Fortunately the contractor persevered."*

The assessor checked the box indicating that he would support the award of another federal contract to my firm of a similar size and magnitude.

That review felt like the best one I ever received in my life. It marked the end of a great battle, a struggle that almost sank my firm, ruined my livelihood, and destroyed my reputation.

If I had not persevered through this category 6 storm, I would have damaged many lives, and many companies working for me would have been hurt financially. My dedicated crew would have lost jobs in a terrible economy if I failed.

Most likely, I would have also filed bankruptcy on the business. It surely would have been taken over by a 3rd party and run into the ground. After that would come personal bankruptcy and even worse: being disbarred as a federal contractor. The DOL probably would have filed charges against me. Who knows what other calamities I would have faced? To complete this job was the equivalent of climbing Mt. Everest without safety gear.

That June, I showed my appreciation to my team again by unfreezing their salaries and offering pay increases. Without them, I could not have endured. Throughout the rest of the year, PKS continued to manage the bank and pay down debt. The bonding company loosened their grip on me, and we won new projects, including one near and dear to my heart: repairing walkways in and around the Arlington National Cemetery Amphitheater and the home of the Tomb of the Unknown Soldier. Getting that job was a proud moment for me. Someone even snapped a photo of the president walking over our newly completed work.

We also took time to bid another project with the same agency that nearly killed my firm at West Palm. Believe it or not, we won it. We completed the project in 90 days, on time and on budget. One government official said off the record to my superintendent, "Tell your boss his reputation is restored. You have done a great job." My superintendent didn't know what that meant, but I did. We had fried another fish. Completing that work was a very important milestone for me.

While wrapping up the year-end in 2014, with my accountants and underwriters busy crunching our financials, I received an email from my bonding agent's underwriter. "Congratulations! I saw your statement." That message meant a lot to me. I felt proud, happy, and sad at the same time. My emotions were high. All things considered, I never saw the money I would have earned anyway. That would have compounded the pain I felt if I physically touched it.

By the same token, my experiences early in life gave me the motivation to survive. I definitely didn't want to go back to that place. I had worked too hard for that. So failure was never an option. In actuality, I lost three years of my life to a disaster that should never have happened. But I gained a lifetime of experience and confidence because of it.

Closing Thoughts...

Sean P. Jensen

Aloha

Goodbye

Sean P. Jensen

BY June of 2014, Polu Kai Services recovered and got back into the black. My team and I didn't quit. PKS is near its 2011 book value, and it still owes some money on the line. We are half the size, but we are sailing true in calmer waters. There are no storms on the horizon. I am relaxed, just as I was coming home from the hurricanes in '04 when I needed sleep. I took 3 weeks off in December and January. I have recouped my strength and prepared for my next adventure.

I have as humbly as possible shared this story. I have told you about my success and my trials, as well as the reasoning and tactics I used along the way to overcome those trials. The Polu Kai story is compelling, but statistics are proof. I mentioned earlier that Polu Kai Services, upon its founding and incorporation in 2003, had a starting bank balance of $1,600 dollars. Since then, PKS has captured and signed contracts with the government and other agencies valued near three quarters of a billion dollars over the course of s13 years.

No, I haven't earned a billion dollars, but that's the kind of opportunity every one of those contracts brings. Life is opportunity. That kind of accomplishment required us to compete and work our tails off. The opportunity and capacity for success has been incredible. Our company has faced off against the top competitors in the country and won many times.

Since our inception as a firm, PKS has created thousands of jobs: temporary, part-time, full-time, and plenty with our subcontractors and vendors. Our company put people to work. Our average retention time for my staff is 5 years. Turnover is very low. And the work our firm has completed has created many opportunities to hire for our firm, as well as our vendors and subcontractors. Since we are law-abiding, tax-paying citizens, we know that our taxes at the federal, state, and local level help the economy, especially now, when the nation needs small economic engines like my firm.

Polu Kai was named to the *Inc. 500* magazine's top 500 fastest growing 500 private companies for 4 consecutive years. The first year we were listed in the top 5000. PKS was also named one of the top 50 minority businesses in the country by *MBE* magazine during that same period. PKS was recently named one of the top minority businesses in the Washington DC metropolitan area by the *Washington Business Journal* in early 2015.

We have completed projects in over 40 states and accomplished tasks off the continental US in places like Hawaii, Afghanistan, Cuba, Puerto Rico, and the Virgin Islands.

And Polu Kai has given back to our communities, donating over $100,000 to charities the last 7 years. These organizations are varied: church groups, food banks, veterans' organizations, Make a Wish, and Toys for Tots. My team also has donated hundreds of volunteer hours to these organizations. And whenever possible, PKS hires disabled, wounded warriors.

Finally, with that $1,600 I first deposited, Polu Kai managed to gross over $170,000,000 over the last 7 years. Keeping it is another story all together. That's not a bad return for a guy who started on his back porch. I still live in the same home my wife and I bought after I left the Marines, and I still drive a Ford. I am proud of our humble accomplishments.

Mahalo

Thanks

Sean P. Jensen

I will do my best to acknowledge all of the people in my life who inspired me to undertake this book. To quote a friend, "Invisible does not mean unimportant" (Robbie Grayson). I want all of my partners, friends, family, and associates to know that if your name is not mentioned, I am still eternally thankful for your presence in my life. So many people have impacted and influenced my life in a positive way! The people and organizations thanked below are in no particular order.

Before anyone else, I thank my wife of 19 years for taking a chance on a young Marine, and my daughter, who will graduate college this year. She has developed into a fine, principled young lady.

Then I'd like to thank my extended family, beginning with Mr. Gordon Ayers - rest in peace, Hiram; Mr. Paul Witkus and Mr. Johnny "V" Vrotsos; Mr. Richard Vrotsos - rest in peace. I never got a chance to know you; one day we will catch up on the other side. To Kim, Samantha, Cassie, Becky, Tyler, and Makalah - I will always be a phone call away. I promised Poppa. David Ayers and family – you're true sailors all. To the kids I never expected but gratefully accepted as my own for the smiles and laughter they gave me - David G., Chris H., and Justin B. (the sons); Julia J. (heathen number 2, a.k.a. Surround Sound); Justin S. (don't tow my car, dude); Isaac (The Next PM of Australia); and all of the others that ate my food and drank my beer. This book is for you, too. I can't wait to see where you all go in life. I thank my mom and dad, who adopted three desperate children. I'd also like to send a special thanks to my brother, Mark Jensen, for keeping the phone lines open.

I owe sincere thanks to the United States Marine Corps, which gave me training and discipline along with great mentors. To my fellow Marines, Semper Fi. SSGT Featherston, here's a special thanks from Jenky. Major Fred Mock, USMC Ret., I'm going Hollywood, sir. Mr. Duane O 'Barr and Ms. Sally Meckle - thanks for translating civilian to jarhead. I gratefully acknowledge the members of the United States Armed forces, including all of the veterans past and present who defended our right to be free. I also thank the government civilians who tirelessly serve the US taxpayer.

Thank you to the entire staff of Polu Kai Services, LLC, my family and friends who never gave up in uncertain times. Specifically, thanks to Ms. Dawn Kelly Wall, my secret weapon; Mr. Randy Sosa, my Cuban ambassador; Mr. Aaron Baltimore, no parachute required; Mr. John Lang, who says I'm green (Johnny Hazmat); Ms. Gail "no fear" Holland, Mr. Dan Schlosser, the weatherman; Lt. Col. Brian Rogers, USA, Ret., a true colonel; and Ms. Jeanne Germaise, no job too small ("You need that by when?")

I sincerely thank all of my friends: Mr. and Mrs. John Nocera (whatever happens, it's not my fault); Mr. Jack Beecher, the example; Mr. Scott Mahorsky, my brother; Sgt. Maj. Don Morse, USA, Ret. (Don't call me sir!); Mr. John Manfredonia, Esq., the only lawyer I ever enjoyed paying; Mr. Eric Brown, Devil Dog; the Honorable Dr. Ray Jardine, who is an inspiration to veterans and the Hawaiian people (Mahalo Nui Loa); the Honorable Mr. Ray Fatz, the greybeard; Ms. Cheryl Drum, the admiral's daughter; Mr. Tim Caldwell; Mr. Stacey Turner, to whom I owe thanks for letting me finish what I started; Mr. Al Negron – (The VA misses your leadership); Dave and Cathy Perry, who are true friends; Mr. Robert Wilson – (I climbed out of that ditch!); Mr. David Carrol – (Look, I'm a roofer!); Lt. Col. Don Lauzon, USA Ret., Sherman to Grant; Mr. Dan Ward – (Inspired leadership knows no boundaries); Mr. Mark Healy and Mr. Brent Tenney, who both gave me knowledge and perspective on misunderstood topics; Ms. Carol Cromer ("You can only have 5%") - thanks for giving PKS a chance! To my executive assistants through the years: Ms. Valerie Zambrana, Ms. Cynthia DeJesus, Ms. Laura Johnson-Webb, and Ms. Angela Jackson – thank you ladies for keeping me straight in my adventures. Mrs. Barbara Parks, thanks for sweet-talking the lumber yard. Mr. William "Billy" Tyree, Jr., this CEO stuff is not hard at all; I'm glad you didn't tell me the truth. Mr. Mark Boller and Douglas "Doug" Hamilton, thanks for the intro to small business. Leonard Loebach, PhD, you're the chairman of the unofficial board. Mr. Jim Weber, thanks for showing me how to treat a subcontractor right. And to Dave and Rebecca Tax and the staff of The Beach Shack, thanks for adopting my firm.

I'd also like to offer a most grateful thanks to the following people. Without them, this book would not have been possible: my editor, Mark Baird, CEO of Hire Patriots; my publisher, Traitmarker Books, run by Robbie and Sharilyn Grayson, and my photographer; Keoni K of KEONIK Photography.

I thank the good Lord, who programmed me with no limitations. Inside me, I know there will be more opportunities to break another barrier or to discover an unwritten rule for success tomorrow. I'm grateful for the ability to impact the economy around me by providing good pay and good jobs for hardworking people trying to get ahead in life.

Finally, I am grateful for the opportunity to share this story with you.

These chapters of my life are over now. I will have this book as a memory. I'm not sure how the whole story of my life is going to end, because I am writing a new pieces of that life story every day. New chapters lie ahead. After all, I am only 42 as I write this. Who knows for sure what else I'll do? Maybe I will be able to share more stories with you in the future.

My life has been an incredible journey so far. I hope that you never have to endure the hard things I have. For those of you who have been through worse, I hope never to experience your pain and agony. Like I said, I am a firm believer in destiny. I think you can change your destiny by being positive, by doing the right thing, and by making the right decision at the right time.

I wish you all of the best in life!

Sean

Sean P. Jensen

Appendix

Polu Kai in the News

http://www.polukaiservices.com/
http://www.wsj.com/articles/SB10001424052748703806304576235571264260618
https://www.linkedin.com/company/polu-kai-services
https://www.facebook.com/pages/Polu-Kai-Services-LLC/110504412351935
https://twitter.com/polukaiservices
http://www.gpo.gov/fdsys/pkg/USCOURTS-laed-2_06-cv-10708
http://www.asbca.mil/Decisions/2014/58726,%2058795%20Polu%20Kai%20Services,%20LLC%20 7.29.14.pdf
http://www.prnewswire.com/news-releases/polu-kai-services-awarded-usace-huntsville-district-multiple-award-task-order-contract-matoc-262381911.html
https://www.fbo.gov/index2?s=opportunity&mode=form&id=58ae9ccb17a511661d-f4e110b053f04b&tab=core&tabmode=list&print_preview=1
http://www.bizjournals.com/washington/prnewswire/press_releases/Virginia/2014/06/09/PH44365
http://www.bizjournals.com/washington/news/2011/08/23/dc-maryland-and-virginia-land-59.html
http://www.bizjournals.com/washington/prnewswire/press_releases/Virginia/2012/08/29/PH64989
http://www.bizjournals.com/washington/prnewswire/press_releases/Virginia/2012/09/21/PH78945
http://www.bizjournals.com/washington/subscriber-only/2015/02/27/minority-owned-companies.html
http://www.prnewswire.com/news-releases/polu-kai-services-named-to-prestigious-inc-5005000-for-fourth-consecutive-year-167841245.html
http://www.prnewswire.com/news-releases/polu-kai-services-named-to-prestigious-inc-5005000-for-second-consecutive-year-101809913.html
http://www.prweb.com/releases/2011/9/prweb4245824.htm
http://naturalresources.house.gov/oversight/coalregsdocs.htm
http://docs.naturalresources.house.gov/Oversight/CoalRegs/Docs-PoluKaiServices.pdf
http://www.hahnlaw.com/wp-content/uploads/2015/02/987.pdf
http://www.army.mil/article/133922/Arlington_National_Cemetery_s_Welcome_Center_renovations_set_to_start_later_this_month/
http://mediamatters.org/research/2012/05/24/fox-serves-as-mouthpiece-for-mountaintop-mining/183995
http://www.sameposts.org/directory_companies/269
http://www.epa.gov/oig/reports/2011/20110803-11-R-0431.pdf
http://www.hawaiireporter.com/honolulu-district-awards-multiple-award-task-order-contract-that-will-help-service-disabled-veteran-owned-small-businesses
http://www.examiner.com/article/operation-dragoon-anniversary-commemoration
http://www.sdvconference.com/members/
http://government-contracts.findthebest.com/l/8205039/Polu-Kai-Services-Llc-Department-of-Veterans-Affairs-VA248C1473
http://technews.tmcnet.com/news/2012/10/13/6648858.htm

(cont.)

http://secure.sameposts.org/franchises/south-florida/blogs/2014-industry-day-presentations
http://www.epa.gov/oamcinc1/conference/booklet.pdf
http://www.epa.gov/region4/superfund/images/nplmedia/pdfs/towchemflfax122013.pdf
http://government-contractors.findthebest.com/l/69031/Polu-Kai-Services-Llc-in-Falls-Church-VA
http://www.washingtonpost.com/business/capitalbusiness/washington-area-federal-contract-awards/2013/07/03/cdbd94ee-e342-11e2-aef3-339619eab080_story.html
http://www.prnewswire.com/news-releases/polu-kai-services-awarded-us-navy-multiple-award-construction-contract-macc-170702616.html
https://www.flickr.com/photos/navfac/7209636254/
http://www.quanticosentryonline.com/news/article_4a81fc34-eba1-57be-8b48-914a32f3b462.html
http://www.nrlrc.net/content/enews/view.aspx?nid=9
http://www.joplinglobe.com/news/local_news/hospital-being-razed/article_980be1f1-71b9-5297-9495-87b086e2d064.html
http://www.futurenetgroup.com/pdf/FutureNet%20Nesho%20Project.pdf
http://www.washingtonexaminer.com/interior-ig-kept-documents-from-congress-out-of-respect-for-interior-department/article/2541910
http://naturalresources.house.gov/oversight/coalregsdocs.htm
http://www.washingtontimes.com/news/2013/dec/30/government-tried-change-coal-regulation-numbers-pr/
http://www.novasame.org/presentations/2012-SBGC-Beecher.ppt
https://www.google.com/url?sa=t&rct=j&q=&esrc=s&source=web&cd=4&ved=0C-C8QFjAD&url=http%3A%2F%2Fmenrec.com%2Fscandal-obama-officials-caught-pressuring-contractors-to-fudge-job-loss-numbers%2F&ei=ScgmVcffIIOusAWjy4HICg&usg=AFQjCNHAuUK-bGPZi4oiJrALv6i1nLYdFqA
https://www.google.com/url?sa=t&rct=j&q=&esrc=s&source=web&cd=2&ved=0C-CUQFjAB&url=http%3A%2F%2Fbeforeitsnews.com%2Fopinion-conservative%2F2014%2F01%-2Fobama-fired-contractor-that-refused-to-fake-number-of-jobs-lost-due-to-policies-2787058.html&ei=ScgmVcffIIOusAWjy4HICg&usg=AFQjCNGutJ7sz3slQeliigvvc45mV-zeiQ
https://www.google.com/url?sa=t&rct=j&q=&esrc=s&source=web&cd=1&ved=0C-B4QFjAA&url=http%3A%2F%2Ffreebeacon.com%2Fnational-security%2Fnot-the-real-world%2F&ei=ScgmVcffIIOusAWjy4HICg&usg=AFQjCNGCaLpw748kv-AXVv94FptMTXLSrw
https://www.google.com/url?sa=t&rct=j&q=&esrc=s&source=web&cd=7&ved=0CE-MQFjAG&url=http%3A%2F%2Fissuu.com%2Ffcnp%2Fdocs%2F12-24-09%2F11&ei=R8omVaWD-B4jxsAW8jIG4CQ&usg=AFQjCNEcRhoh1o3sGbkbAzC1QalFLXXIMA

CPSIA information can be obtained
at www.ICGtesting.com
Printed in the USA
FFOW01n1507191215
19633FF